AIRPORT BUILDERS

AIRPORT BUILDERS

MARCUS BINNEY

Aⁱⁱⁱⁱ ACADEMY EDITIONS

Acknowledgements

This book benefits substantially from material supplied by the architects of the airport terminals illustrated and the airport authorities who commissioned the projects; to all of them I extend grateful thanks. Supplementary information on the subject may be obtained from the following titles: *Building for Air Travel: Architecture and Design for Commercial Aviation*, edited by John Zukowsky, 1996; *Airport Terminals*, by Christopher Blow, first published in 1991; and *The Modern Terminal*, by Brian Edwards, 1998. Other recent books in the field are *The World's Airports* by Yoichi Arai, 1996, and *Airport*, 1997. Architectural and aviation magazines are also a key source of information; likewise, *The Arup Journal* and *Arup Focus*, published by engineers Ove Arup & Partners.

Special thanks are due to Dennis Sharp, Michael Spens and to Lufthansa for assistance in visiting new terminals in Germany. Finally, my thanks are due to Maggie Toy, senior publishing editor, to Mariangela Palazzi-Williams for efficiently handling all aspects of production, to Lucy Isenberg for copy editing and Iona Spens and Francesca Wisniewska for dealing with the proofs. Design has been in the capable hands of Mario Bettella and Andrea Bettella at Artmedia.

Photographic credits

All photographs are courtesy of the architects or from the Architectural Press archive, unless stated otherwise; every effort has been made to locate sources and credit material but in the very few cases where this has not been possible our apologies are extended: A. Buonomo pp 202; © Advanced Media Design pp 44; Airphotos International pp108; Architekturfotografie © Bernadette Grimmenstein pp 90; Arup Photographic Library pp 20 centre, 32, 35; Bartenbach pp 19 above; © Klaus Frahm pp 88, 92, 93, 94 above; Carl Dalio pp19 centre, 77; Chris Gascoigne pp 145 centre; Chuck Choi pp 16; Dean Sharr pp 212; Dennis Gilbert pp 17, 154, 155 above; Doormoolen pp 89, 94 below; Duccio Malagamba pp 198, 199; Eamonn O'Mahony pp 145 below; Jack Pottle / Esto pp 165; John Nye pp 17 left, 104, 105; John Linden pp 145 above; Kawatetsu pp114 below, Ken Kirkwood pp 150-1, 152; Loo Keng Yip pp 120, 123, 124, 125, 126, 127; M. Green pp 217 below; Nick Merrick © Hedrick Blessing pp 8, 71, 72; Paul Maurer pp 110, 172, 178, 180, 181; Paul Ott pp 84, 86, 87; R. Bryant pp 208; Raimondo di Egidio pp 2, 25 above, 130, 132, 134, 135; Richard Davies pp 148, 155 below; Richard Latoff pp 25 centre, 214; Rion Rizzo pp 19 below; Ron Johnson pp 74 centre; S. Ishida pp 114 above, 116; Susuma Shingu pp 118 below; Tanja Belgrado Photography pp 40, 41. 42, 43; Thierry Prieur & Christophe Valtin pp 170; Tomio Ohashi pp 121; Toshimaru Kitasima pp 117 above left; W.D.Gericke pp 206, 209 above right, 210, 211; Werner Hennies pp 158, 160, 162; Yoshio Hata pp 112; Yutaka Kinumaki pp 117 above right, 118 above.

Cover: Frankfurt Airport, Terminal 2, Germany, JSK Perkins & Will
Frontispiece: McCarran Airport, Satellite D, Las Vegas, Nevada, Leo A Daly and Tate & Snyder

First published in Great Britain in 1999 by
ACADEMY EDITIONS

A division of
JOHN WILEY & SONS
Baffins Lane
Chichester
West Sussex PO19 1UD

ISBN: 0-471-98445-0

Other Wiley Editorial Offices
New York • Weinheim • Brisbane • Singapore • Toronto

Printed and bound in Italy

CONTENTS

PREFACE

There will have been so many air terminals built in the 1990s, ever bigger, more ambitious and often more beautiful, that wary as one might be of the short-sighted bias that makes us mistake history's ripples for waves, we have good reason to believe that this decade will leave a lasting mark on the history of this built form. From an architectural standpoint, it may very well be regarded as 'the age of air terminals', as other periods were 'the age of railway stations' or 'the age of cathedrals', for it has been a time of such keen interest in an area that has facilitated the expression of new ideas and, on occasion, given form to older ideas that could not be applied elsewhere.

Obviously, many terminals were built before the nineties, some of which were outstanding architectural events: first and foremost the two American terminals designed by Eero Saarinen – the TWA Terminal Building, JFK Airport, New York (1956–62) and that of Washington Dulles (1958–63). The history of terminal architecture is short, spanning seventy years at the most, but it is dense in experiments and inventions linked to those instigated in the fields of infrastructure, construction and urbanism by airports in general. No doubt there is less invention these days than in the past. Kansai International Airport Terminal in Osaka Bay, for instance, is the realisation of the utopian project outlined by Henry J Gielow and Edward R Armstrong in 1930 of building a 'man-made island to service transatlantic airplanes' and André Lurçat's 1932 plan for 'an airport on the Seine'. Likewise, positioning satellites in the middle of taxiways and providing access to them via underground circulations is a reasonably reduced variation on the utopian project of building an entire airport underground with the free-flowing aircraft traffic above.

In practical and operational terms, it was during the sixties that the most intense conceptual developments took place: Los Angeles, Tampa, Houston, and Kansas City, to mention just the American examples, were all based on new concepts which, flawed and open to criticism as some may have been, greatly inspired present-day developments. The research that was conducted at the time into the organisation of built space, its topology, and the nodes and folds that create its form antici-pated reflections developed by subsequent architects in the light of contemporary philosophical and mathematical ideas. Such research tends to be less daring today; and if the word concept occurs more and more, the number of real concepts that are developed or implemented is actually diminishing.

The focus has shifted. It is now concentrated on the size of the project (sometimes excessive), on the spread of terminals and especially on the harmony that exists between these constructions and ideas in the air at the moment. Terminals respond to trends of thought. Seeped in historical references (however imperfect at times), they are also informed by its complement, geography; they are grounded in commercial and cultural ties across space but also across time. Moreover, founded on an ideology of ubiquity and displacement, they have, paradoxically, recovered a sense of place and roots. Terminals have become more important these days than cultural places such as museums or theatres where societies used to assemble. This is because their space (overly distended, requiring the most advanced technical resources for their construction, at once comfortable and free) is the locus of meeting between what is most universal, mobile and modern – the aeroplane, that dangerous marvel – and what is most primitive – the sense of belonging to a place and the very deep-seated desire to fly, to be somewhere else at once.

Architects have, intuitively, grasped the significance of air terminals, and state authorities, especially in nations with emerging economies, have understood that air terminals are gateways that open their countries to the world, that they serve as relays linking them to the modern community of travel and exchange, and that they are symbols and measures of economic success and development. The last ten years of our century can be compared to the period from 1250 to 1280 that Georges Duby describes as 'the happy times' in *The Age of Cathedrals*. No doubt the works presented in this book will bear out this comparison.

I would like to conclude on a less triumphant, more restrained note, by voicing my concern that terminal architecture will not be victim to the same exhaustion from refinement that Duby observes in mid-thirteenth-century cathedral architecture, 'when French cathedral artists gradually lost their talent for invention'. As the author points out, 'In around 1250 in Saint-Denis the great Pierre de Montreuil was merely refining, not innovating.' Let us hope that we have not yet reached that point and that over and beyond architectural beauty the desire and conditions for invention will continue to subsist in the years to come.

Paul Andreu
(Translated by Gila Walker)

Perkins & Will, Terminal 5, O Hare International Airport, Chicago

NEW DIRECTIONS IN AIRPORT DESIGN

Airports have become key national construction projects around the globe. Every capital, every major provincial city, every region or state, and many small islands, want a spacious, impressive terminal that will give arriving passengers a memorable and welcoming first impression of their country's modernity and sophistication. Correspondingly, most airport architects interpret their brief as an exercise in sleek high-tech design. A few, though the number is increasing, seek to create buildings with a distinct sense of national colour or character.

What sets the airports of the 1990s apart from their predecessors is their prodigious size and cost. The proposed Chicago South Suburban Airport is projected to cost $4,900 million, Denver International cost $3.2 billion and the new Austin–Bergstrom Airport in Texas, $615 million. Likewise, Pittsburgh's new terminal cost $815 million, Detroit's new terminal is forecast at $786 million, the terminal at Shanghai Pudong is budgeted at $317 million, Terminal 2F at Charles de Gaulle, Paris, at 2.5 billion FF, and Oslo's Gardermoen Airport at 20 billion Kroner.

These are very large buildings, designed to impress, and to cope with fast expansion. While simple international rivalry is a spur in itself, still more important has been the freeing of airport authorities from the purse strings of central and local government, allowing them to operate as businesses and raise finance on the basis of expanding revenues.

Airports are now lucrative organisations, raising funds not just through landing fees, but by renting space to a whole range of airside and landside operators, from aircraft maintenance providers and fuel suppliers to freight handlers, and shops, bars, cafes and restaurants, carhire companies, banks and bureaux de change.

Driving the great surge of airport building is the desire to provide for ever increasing numbers of air travellers. Following the example of Charles de Gaulle

Airport at Roissy, more and more airports are building anew: Oslo's Gardermoen on the site of a former military airfield; Austin–Bergstrom in Texas on a former US Airforce base; and the three new island airports in Asia – Kansai, Chek Lap Kok and Seoul's Inchon now under construction, as well as the major new facility at Kuala Lumpur, which opened in 1998, and that at Bangkok, scheduled to open in 2004.

The optimum new airport extends to hundreds of acres with two, three, four or even more runways to allow simultaneous take off and landing. At Denver and Kuala Lumpur, for example, provision is made for four parallel runways.

PLANNERS, DESIGNERS AND BUILDINGS

New airports and major new terminals are colossal undertakings in terms of town and country planning and civil engineering as well as architecture. In the United States of America, particularly, there is an increase in the emergence of large multi-disciplinary practices specialising in airport projects.

HNTB, which has evolved from a civil engineering practice founded in Kansas City in 1914, offers master planning, architectural and engineering services, site selection, feasibility and regulatory studies construction management for airside, terminal and landside facilities for all types of airport – large hubs, small hubs and non-hubs, to use the jargon – as well as specialist services such as noise management, which has become an important issue since the passage of the US Airport Safety and Noise Abatement Act of 1979.

Leo A Daly was founded in Omaha, Nebraska, in 1915 and operates as a multi-disciplinary firm providing planning, architecture, engineering (civil, structural, mechanical and electrical), interior design services and project management with offices around the world. The firm was granted a ten-year contract with the US

The Richard Rogers Partnership, Europier attached to Terminal 1, London Heathrow Airport

Federal Aviation Administration to design air traffic control towers at more than sixty airports.

Hellmuth, Obata & Kassabaum (HOK), established in 1955, provides, *inter alia*, architectural and engineering services, computer systems, as well as store planners, landscape architects, graphic designers and model builders. HOK claims to have ushered in the jet age with its design for the Lambert Terminal, St Louis, in the fifties, and cites its landmark projects as Dallas–Fort Worth: 'one of the first major new airports built in the US', and King Khaled Airport in Saudi Arabia, 'which combines traditional Islamic architecture with contemporary aviation technology'. Since 1984, the firm has completed projects exceeding $7.4 billion of airport construction around the world.

William Nicholas Bodouva + Associates has played a major role in airport design over three decades. Its client list includes Air France, Lufthansa and SAS, in addition to numerous American airlines. In the United Kingdom, Pascall + Watson Architects has built up a large portfolio of airport work since it was first appointed in 1964 to design a flight catering base at London Heathrow, thereafter receiving numerous commissions from the British Airports Authority, including the redesign of Terminal 3's arrival building, major refurbishment of Terminal 2, a check-in extension at London Gatwick and hangars at Stansted and Luton.

The new Gardermoen Airport in Oslo is predominantly the work of a consortium of architects and consulting engineers, Aviaplan AS, established in 1989 to provide a specialist group of professionals capable of preparing a highly qualified entry in the design concept competition for the new airport. It consists of six Scandinavian firms that can draw on the services of some 2,000 employees, and cites transport planning, airport logistics, environmental planning and water supply and sewage among its numerous fields of expertise.

GRAND PLANNING

Airports built on new sites provide opportunities for master planning on a grand scale, matching in both scope and geometric layout the largest 'ideal' town planning projects envisaged in earlier centuries. Architects, engineers and rulers have long been fascinated by the concept of the perfectly planned new town with straight roads, grand axes, grid layouts and great symmetrical buildings approached along imposing avenues and boulevards.

Airports provide the opportunity to realise such ambitions on a scale never seen before. An early example of super grand planning is Kansas City International Airport, laid out in 1968–72 with Kivett and Myers as architects. As originally completed, this consisted of a giant central circle linking three circular, or horseshoe, terminals (four were planned). The whole layout was adapted to the motor car, with gently curving roads and abundant carparking. The principle was that long-term carparking would be easily available immediately in front of each airline's check-in points.

Unfortunately, the concept of 'park and fly' was rendered problematic by the threat of terrorism and the need for much greater security. While Kansas City Airport offered admirably short walking distances from car to plane, it also required a vast number of security check points.

Dallas–Fort Worth (1965–73), by TAMS and HOK, is another early example of grand planning with provision for up to six crescent-shaped terminals set three and three along either side of a broad central road approach – so broad that the central grass reservation is the size of a football pitch. To the uninitiated, the layout can be confusing with its sudden turn offs and loops to terminals on the other side of the road network. From the air, the almost perfectly similar arrangements of runways and taxiways are reminiscent of the discipline of a seventeenth-century formal garden.

The master of grand planning is, appropriately enough, a Frenchman: Paul Andreu, chief architect of Aéroports de Paris. His *chef-d'oeuvre* – and life's work – is the new Charles de Gaulle Airport at Roissy, north-east of Paris. The design began with Terminal 1, which was conceived as a perfectly circular drum surrounded by seven island satellites linked by walkways beneath the aprons. Andreu then embarked on the much grander project for Terminal 2.

The basis of the concept for the second terminal is the French love of a grand axis – manifested in the Champs Elysées rising to the Arc de Triomphe and now continued to the Grande Arche de La Défense. Andreu develops this theme in two commanding ways. First, by bisecting his main axis with a second axis, for trains rather than cars, thus giving equal symbolic importance to the two means of approach: road and rail. The foresight in planning and achieving such perfection is immense, when so many other pressures are brought to bear on airport land over a long period.

Second, Andreu adds an almost Baroque flourish by relinquishing pure straight lines and right angles in favour of designing the terminals in matching pairs to form a succession of ovals. While Louis XIV was required to spend a fortune on levelling the ground at Versailles to create the perfect *tabula rasa* to accommodate his grand symmetrical layout, Andreu had the advantage of a site that consisted of flat, open former farmland. Nonetheless, the need to interweave different levels for trains and motor vehicles, as well as separate drop-off points for departures and arrivals, vastly increased the complexity of the overall design, introducing a series of Los Angeles style elevated freeways with fast lanes continuing through on the main axis, and loop roads serving each pair of terminals. In a display of sheer virtuosity, Andreu chose to build the focal point of the layout, a torpedo-shaped hotel, at the point where it would be most challenging to set the foundations – over the tracks of the new station. Significantly, he was also the creative genius behind the mile-long terminal at Kansai International Airport, another project laid out on a grand scale with a powerful axis running through the building like a laser beam (the commission to design the building went to Renzo Piano).

No less imposing than his designs for Charles de Gaulle are Andreu's plans for Shanghai-Pudong, another airport laid out on either side of a grand ceremonial approach road. The masterplan provides for four Kansai-style terminals, each with a long departure concourse extending on either side of the main building. Andreu's plans show planes as neatly lined up as fighter aircraft at a military aerodrome. On either side, taxiways and runways are laid out almost as mirror images – the difference being that they are staggered and thus clearly distinct from the air, each with one end close to the centre of the airport complex. Intriguingly, the plan is a rare example of Andreu designing off-grid, with the main approach road set at an angle until it straightens out into a central ceremonial way on the scale of New Delhi. In the first phase, just one of the four proposed terminals is being built. Whether the airport authorities will follow Andreu's original masterplan as closely as that of Charles de Gaulle remains an open question.

The stupendous growth rates of the Asian 'tiger' economies in the late 1980s and early 1990s were the impetus behind a series of highly ambitious plans for new airports, with Chek Lap Kok, opened in July 1998, boasting the largest airport terminal in the world. In the same month, Kuala Lumpur's ambitious new airport also became operational. This is another example of a spectacular grand layout, which, from a bird's-eye view, is strangely reminiscent of a vast eighteenth-century parterre. Again, the airport was planned with a grand central axial approach accommodating twin terminals on either side and four propeller-shaped island satellites. In the initial phase of construction, only one terminal and one satellite have been built, but these are on a colossal scale, and in themselves constitute one of the largest airports in the region. Here again, roads are planned in perfect symmetry with inner and outer loops and four runways, three parallel but staggered, and one extended runway set at right angles.

In terms of sheer scale, the most ambitious building proposal of all was for Seoul's new island airport at Inchon. The original masterplan shows a grid layout equal in size to a large town with office blocks and residential buildings interspersed with ornamental gardens and formally planted woodland. As in a grand Baroque or classical layout there are intersecting avenues, rond points and rectangular basins of water. The main axis was to be extended as a strongly architectural peninsula into the sea. The whole chequer board layout is contained within a vast egg-shaped ring road and continued at the far end by the airport proper with a car-park, followed by a landmark gateway building designed by the Terry Farrell Partnership, and then a crescent-shaped terminal by Fentress Bradburn, with two finger piers.

In the grand plan, the airport layout was to be further extended by a succession of four island terminals linked by an underground shuttle train. It was intended that the whole airport be built in four phases, each phase accommodating a new runway. The final layout was to achieve an unsurpassed degree of mirror symmetry as a result of the precise alignment of the runways. With the onset of the Asian recession, the phasing of the masterplan is uncertain but the Farrell gateway and the Fentress Bradburn terminal are under construction with a view to opening in time for the World Cup in Korea in 2002.

In North America, the most ambitious of the new layouts can be seen at Denver. Again, this is a new site laid out symmetrically along a main axis with a network of elevated roads encircling the terminal. So perfect is the symmetry that, once inside, people are warned to remember where they parked their car. Here the freeway approaches at right angles before turning on its axis to reach the terminal. Beyond the departure halls the axis is continued by the people mover train which runs under the aprons to serve three successive island concourses.

REACHING THE AIRPORT

While fast, easy land access is essential to any airport, travelling distances for passengers and personnel are increasing. The need for ever larger sites and the noise generated by increasing numbers of aircraft mean that the optimum site for new airports is usually far out of town. Fewer major airports are now close to city centres. The most famous, Hong Kong's Kai Tak, with its descent among the tower blocks (breathtaking or hair-raising according to the individual point of view) closed in July 1998. Washington National remains, but new airports are being built on more distant sites where aircraft noise in particular will disturb fewer people.

From London Heathrow a new high-speed fifteen-minute link runs four times an hour to London's Paddington Station, though there is, as yet, no prospect of a direct connection to trains running west on Brunel's Great Western Line to Bristol, which passes barely two miles to the north of the airport. In Hong Kong, an express line has been built to serve the new Chek Lap Kok Airport on the island of Lantau. Fast trains take just twenty-three minutes from downtown, where passengers may also check in their baggage. In Norway, passengers travelling to and from Oslo's new Gardermoen Airport may take a new nineteen-minute high-speed train, having checked their luggage in at Oslo's central station. In Japan, the new island airport of Kansai, serving the cities of Osaka and Kobe, benefits from a new railway line, approached along a viaduct across the bay. Passengers may use a range of express trains or take the slower but extraordinary midnight-blue rocket-like Rapi:t [sic] train which covers the 42.8 kilometre journey at a more stately pace.

As a result of the competitive nature of airlines and railways in the United Kingdom, connections between train and plane are often awkward. The obvious exception is Gatwick, which from its origin in the 1930s stood on the main London to Brighton line, with its own station and direct connections to London's Victoria Station, and now also to London Bridge,

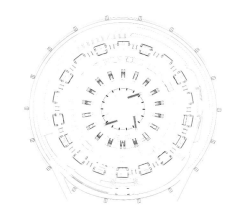

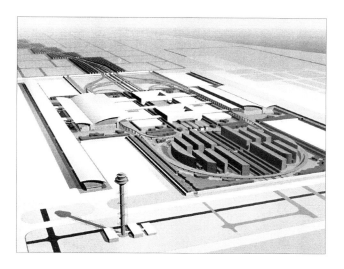

ABOVE: Aéroports de Paris, Charles de Gaulle Airport, Terminal 1, Roissy, Paris plan; CENTRE: Aéroports de Paris, Pudong Airport, Shanghai; BELOW: Terry Farrell & Partners, Inchon Transportation Centre, Seoul; OVERLEAF: CW Fentress, JH Bradburn and Associates, Denver International Airport, Colorado

Blackfriars, King's Cross and Charing Cross.

At Charles de Gaulle, the TGV now runs through the airport connecting it with north, south and eastern France as well as Germany, Belgium and Holland.

In the United States, good airport links have traditionally meant fast access to nearby freeways and interstate highways (for example, Washington Dulles is approached along its own landscaped freeway), but in Europe, and increasingly in Asia where major airports serve densely populated cities, there is equal emphasis on good public transport connections.

The best served airports offer more than a direct fast rail link or metro to the neighbouring city, since they stand astride major intercity rail links; Holland's Schipol and Zurich's Kloten Airport are outstanding examples. Schipol has regular main line services connecting with cities all over Holland and beyond. From Kloten it is just ten minutes to the city's Hauptbahnhof, which boasts rail connections all over Switzerland and Europe. At Geneva, several long distance expresses leave the airport every hour for major European destinations, while Frankfurt's busy airport is less than fifteen minutes' ride to the city's main station and train services all over Europe.

The alternative to a fast dedicated link is connection to a city's metro service. Inevitably, this entails longer journey times involving more frequent stops but it is cheaper, often considerably so, offering a wider range of destinations and possible savings in onward travel time and expense. London Heathrow connects to the whole of the large London Underground network, though journey times to central London of forty-five to sixty minutes are slow. Munich offers a metro service beginning through green fields and reaching the city centre in half an hour.

LANDMARKS

The new terminals are designed as landmark buildings and are frequently symbolic in shape. The time when the height of terminals had to be low in order to avoid creating a hazard to approaching aircraft is long past – many airport buildings are the equivalent of seven, eight, or more storeys high, which makes them monumental structures that cannot be missed on any approach road; that was until the demand for carparking grew to such an extent that some terminals are virtually concealed by the multi-storey car parks in front of them.

ONE TERMINAL OR SEVERAL?

The usual means of providing for increasing passenger numbers is to add new terminals or extensions to existing facilities. Flights are commonly divided between domestic and international terminals; domestic, European and international terminals (as at Barcelona Airport); or, as is common in the United States, individual airlines or groups of airlines build their own terminals. Examples are United Airlines' terminal at O'Hare International Airport, Chicago; Saarinen's famous TWA terminal at New York's JFK Airport, and now the combined terminal for Air France, Korean Airlines, JAL and Lufthansa.

Some major new airports have set out to counter this trend towards on-site fragmentation by providing a single large terminal for all flights. Munich Airport, which opened in 1992, is a key example. Both departures and arrivals are at ground level making the building almost as long as that at Kansai. The advantage, for passengers who know (or quickly find) the right entrance for their airline, is that walking distances can be significantly reduced from pavement to departure gate. But if they need to use other facilities or are uncertain of their way, this walk can be oppressive.

Foster's Chek Lap Kok terminal strikes an impressive balance between spaciousness and distance. The walk from the drop-off point is down a gentle ramp providing an overall panorama of all the check-in islands. Beyond, the shopping areas are as easy to progress through as to dally in, and when the great long vista opens up to the distant gates (the ultimate *salle des pas perdus*), there are moving walkways as well as a shuttle train to speed passengers on their way.

ONE AIRPORT OR MORE?

Chicago's O'Hare has long held the record as the busiest airport in the world, though Atlanta runs it a close second. Since O'Hare cannot expand to meet the needs of the Chicago area, an even more massive South Suburban Airport is planned. In addition, there is the smaller Chicago Midway, closer to the city centre. New York boasts three major airports: JFK and Newark New Jersey run level, with La Guardia not far behind in terms of passenger numbers. In London, British Airways now runs more flights out of Gatwick than Heathrow. Growth is slower at Stansted and London City but Luton Airport is expanding fast thanks to a cheap flights policy. In Paris, the airports authority closed

William Nicholas Bodouva + Associates, La Guardia Airport, New York

Aéroports de Paris, Charles de Gaulle Airport, Roissy, Terminal 1

down Le Bourget when Charles de Gaulle Airport opened, and drastically reduced flights to Orly on the south side of Paris, though it was closer to the city and more convenient for many travellers. Now Orly is growing again. Busy Milan has two airports – Lineate and Malpensa – with a new L2,200 billion hub opened in 1998, a reflection of the flourishing commercial life of the city.

Airport managers and governments like the prestige afforded by a monumental airport, and there are obvious advantages, in terms of connections, in all flights departing from one airport. But in an increasingly market-led business, passenger convenience is still more important, and those living on one side of a great conurbation such as Chicago, London, Milan, New York or Paris can find themselves spending much begrudged time getting to an airport on the other side. Dominating airports such as Heathrow can be subject to delays at peak periods, just when many want to make a fast getaway or landing, with planes stacked up in the sky or waiting for a take-off slot.

Location is important. Many business travellers start their journey from home. London Stansted with its connections into Liverpool Street may be convenient for businessmen arriving from the Continent, whose destination is the City, but its distant site makes it much less accessible for the populous residential areas south and west of London.

ONE LEVEL OR TWO?

Most new airports have arrivals and departures on separate levels – notable exceptions are London Stansted (where arrivals and departures share the same concourse) and Barcelona where both arrivals and departures are at ground level (at Stansted the main level is raised, involving a walk up a ramp for those who use the carparking outside).

The dominant pattern around the world is for an upper-level departures hall, approached by an elevated roadway, and a ground level arrivals hall. As most jetliners have doorways 6 metres or more above the ground, departing passengers need have no stairs or escalators to ascend and can walk on the level to the departure gate (or descend), and then approach the plane down the gentle incline of the airbridge. Equally, while arriving passengers may have a short ascent along the airbridge, they will thereafter descend comfortably by degrees via lifts, stairs or escalators to the baggage reclaim and arrivals hall. Recently, a number of airports have introduced double airbridges providing direct links to both departures and arrivals levels and ensuring that the only walking involved is downhill – down into the plane and down again on disembarking. Such innovative design is incorporated into the new Terminal 2F at Charles de Gaulle and Chek Lap Kok in Hong Kong.

The disadvantage of placing departure facilities over arrivals is that the arrivals level inevitably has less light, particularly in the deep centre of a building. To combat this problem, architects are introducing deep canyons and generous lightwells in the most recent designs for airports to allow daylight to penetrate arrivals levels, including enclosed 'sterile' areas (such as immigration) and baggage reclaim halls as well as meeting areas at the front of a terminal. Examples are the Richard Rogers Partnership designs for Heathrow's Terminal 5 and the new terminal at Madrid. The new international terminal at New York's JFK by William Nicholas Bodouva + Associates, is also designed to allow natural light to flood down through open balconies.

In the United States, the overwhelming majority of

Foster & Partners, Chek Lap Kok Airport, Hong Kong

Foster & Partners, London Stansted Airport

flights are domestic. Where an airport offers no direct international connections, there is often no requirement to separate arriving, departing and transit passengers who can all use the same concourses on a single level, as at the new island satellite terminal in Las Vegas which is purely for domestic flights.

TERMINAL AND SATELLITES

In the past, demands for expansion have often been met by building new terminals for specific purposes – the TWA terminal at New York's JFK, and Terminals 1, 2, 3 and 4 at Heathrow, serving (broadly) British, European, intercontinental airlines and British Airways long-haul flights. In the Far East, at Osaka's Kansai and Hong Kong's Chek Lap Kok, the architects and authorities have tried to reverse this trend by building one vast terminal to accommodate all airlines.

An increase in the number of flights and the size of planes inevitably leads to larger terminals, in some cases achieved by the addition of new piers or satellites with extra gates. The trendsetter here was Atlanta's Hartsfield, with its underground shuttle train providing fast links to four parallel island concourses, a pattern adopted at Denver and proposed for Heathrow's Terminal 5. Architects have also experimented with X-plan island satellites, a configuration held to combine the maximum number of aircraft boarding positions with the shortest walking distances. Other airports use finger piers placed in a U, V or E format and large finger piers serve Charles de Gaulle's new Terminal 2F and are proposed for Seoul's Inchon Airport. As a result of architect Paul Andreu's emphasis on limiting walking distances, Charles de Gaulle's Terminals 2A–D have a mere 50 metres between pavement and plan.

Another format, again minimising walking distances,

is the 'bastion' pier, in plan rather like the spur of a seventeenth-century fortification. Such a design is illustrated by the triangular piers at Barcelona's airport, and pentagonal ones at Jakarta. By grouping planes and passengers in this way it is possible to create a critical mass of potential customers which makes the provision of shops, cafes and bars cost-effective.

With airports figuring as prestigious national projects, whether they serve a capital, major city, or holiday destination, the trend is to make them as large and impressive as possible. Chek Lap Kok opened to a fanfare of publicity announcing it as the largest terminal in the world.

Clearly, architects and airport authorities have to cater both for businessmen and holiday-makers. They must satisfy local people accustomed to arriving for their flights at the last minute and those who wish to spend leisurely time at the airport, or indeed are obliged to do so while waiting for connecting flights. The Hong Kong citizens delighted in last-minute dashes to Kai Tak. Now the new airport is further away but fast trains, or indeed speeding taxis and limousines will help people take advantage of the fact that the departure gates for Cathay Pacific and other locally based airlines are closest to the check-in counters. At Pittsburg, special commuter gates close to check-in serve smaller commuter aircraft. In Brussels, there is a special gate for waiting executive jets, a feature reflecting the city's business and political status.

LIGHT, TRANSPARENCY AND OPENNESS

The essence of air travel is captured by the sensation of bursting through the clouds into sun and blue sky, and a terminal, without natural light or views to the outside world, transforms air travel into a submarine claustrophobic experience, reinforced by the cabin of the plane itself. Abundant daylight is exhilarating, even more so as a sense of bright sun or fast moving clouds, creating patches of shadow and sudden brilliance.

In the field of terminal design, the trend is towards openness and daylight in the 1990s. Having noticed that existing terminals had long tended to pile more and more plant on the roof, cluttering the skyline and eliminating any possibility of daylight entering from above, Foster led the way at Stansted with his floor-to-roof glass, large skylights and a lofty hall without any internal divisions above ground level. Foster & Partners takes transparency a giant step further at Chek Lap Kok Airport, which is surrounded by a continuous 5.5 kilometre wall of glass, providing panoramic views of planes, mountains, sea and ships.

The latest American terminals are even more advanced in the race to build the all-glass palace which glows luminously at night. Newly completed is William Nicholas Bodouva + Associates' international terminal at New York's JFK, a glass-walled and part glass-roofed version of Saarinen's famously sculptural TWA Terminal. In San Francisco, SOM is also building a supremely graceful new international terminal with a huge cantilever glass-clad roof. Earlier but no less impressive examples of transparency are the new international terminal and kilometre-long passenger concourse at Barcelona Airport. Here the Taller de Arquitectura combines lofty ceilings with sheer walls of panoramic glass which create a marvellous sense of spaciousness.

Air travel by its very nature may involve long waits and delays, or last-minute rushes. It can therefore be reassuring to look out of the terminal on to the aprons and runways and observe which planes are arriving and leaving and which are on their stands. Planes are the prime exhibits at any airport and should always be on view. With this in mind, airport facilities should always exploit the view out over the apron. Viewing platforms appeal equally to people seeing off family and friends or greeting them as to day visitors. Airport restaurants that offer a view over the runway, allow patrons the pleasure of relaxing until their incoming flight lands, enabling them to pay the bill or even order dessert or coffee as the plane taxis towards its stand, without feeling the need to rush. Innsbruck Airport, which has a view across the valley of the Inn towards a majestic wall of snow capped mountains, must surely offer the most splendid of airport settings.

TERRACES, CANYONS, BALCONIES AND BRIDGES

Airports are public buildings where people can constitute an irritatingly slow-moving crowd or a lively free-flowing throng. Airports with adequate space can actually be enlivened by large numbers, often hosting a colourful crowd.of many nations.

One way of achieving this meld of numbers and comfort is to allow – indeed encourage – passengers to circulate within a departure hall by placing facilities on several levels. The architect Meinhard von Gerkan has done this to grand effect in his terminals at Stuttgart and Hamburg, where a series of terraces ascends a hill after the manner of the ancient Temple of Palestrina. Versions of Palestrina have entered the canon of Western architecture via numerous practitioners, notably Palladio, who made reconstructions in its image.

Similarly, at Stuttgart and Hamburg airports the far sides of the departure halls are arranged as a series of terraces with shops, bars and restaurants, approached by twin stairways and escalators as in a grand ceremonial building. The tiered effect is rather like a British wedding cake, with people seated at tables, sometimes under umbrellas (purely decorative), eating at a variety of restaurants and cafes as they might in a piazza. At Stuttgart the lower terrace extends around the side, providing space for those who want to relax away from other people. Both airports have high-level open-air terraces overlooking the runway. At Hamburg, tables and chairs are set out by the self-service cafeteria; at Stuttgart the terrace is enhanced by a display of historic aircraft, for which an entry fee is charged.

Renzo Piano introduced a great canyon at Kansai Airport, enabling daylight to penetrate the building deep down. This design concept has been developed further by the Richard Rogers Partnership in its designs for Heathrow's Terminal 5 and also its competition winning scheme for a new Madrid terminal. Here, the baggage reclaim is placed at the bottom of the canyon allowing it to be lit naturally. Above, the canyon will be crossed by a series of bridges leading from the check-in area to security and passport control.

NATIONAL OR INTERNATIONAL?

World travel will lose some of its glamour if major air terminals become indistinguishable. Intriguing therefore are the architects who go against the trend. Most memorable is Rafael Moneo. His San Pablo Airport, Seville, is monumental: its massive beehive dome is an echo of Moorish architecture. Equally striking is Cesar Pelli's new terminal at Washington National, complete with long perspectives of pointed arches. At Doha International Airport, Fentress Bradburn introduced towers based on traditional Qatari wind towers, while at Oslo's new Gardermoen, the Norwegian government insisted on the use of indigenous wood rather than steel for the roof with the aim of creating a distinctively Norwegian character. At Chattanooga the architects sought to evoke the Classicism of Beaux-Arts railway stations, reflecting the city's importance as a railway junction.

METAPHORS FOR FLIGHT

In their designs for new terminals, architects make frequent visual references to the great railway stations of the nineteenth-century, admiring them not only for their impressive spans and metal and glass construction but as icons of travel. Many designs also make explicit or implicit references to flight, both of birds and planes. Flight is evoked generally by curved and waving roofs (often symmetrical to suggest wings), by lightness of construction and by reference to aircraft building techniques – the struts of biplanes, the lattice work construction of fuselages.

Roofs, therefore, are the key to the architecture of the new generation of air terminals, often seeming to float on walls of glass. One of the most extraordinary examples is the new SOM international terminal at San Francisco, now under construction. Here, the roof is cantilevered out in two directions from the central supports like the wings of a bird.

Santiago Calatrava, who has designed the new terminal under construction in Bilbao, refers to the roof as 'the fifth facade'. Here it will be all the more prominent as the terminal can be seen from the surrounding hills. Calatrava's dramatic free-form roof soars upwards. Another metaphor for flight, Terry Farrell's Transportation Centre for Inchon Airport, Seoul, began as an allegory for a bird – the long-necked crane which in Korea has strong symbolic associations. Curt Fentress, who is designing the adjoining Terminal 1, states that his new roof will 'symbolically reflect the aerodynamic shapes of planes'. By contrast, from the air, Foster's new Chek Lap Kok terminal is strongly suggestive of a model plane or glider, with a long straight fuselage and swept-back tail.

For those with a taste for *architecture parlante* –

ABOVE: Von Gerkan • Marg & Partner, Stuttgart Airport; CENTRE: CW Fentress, JH Bradburn and Associates, Doha Airport, Quatar; BELOW: Gensler, Chattanooga Airport

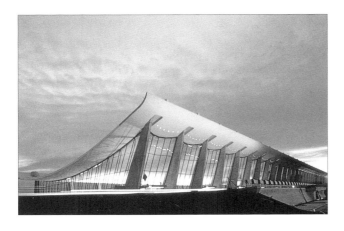

ABOVE: S.O.M. Washington Dulles Airport; CENTRE: Ricardo Bofill, Taller de Arquitectura, Barcelona Airport; BELOW: Von Gerkan • Marg & Partner, Hamburg Airport

architecture which proclaims its purpose – Nicholas Grimshaw's pier 4A at London Heathrow is based on the vocabulary of aircraft design: a rounded 'fuselage', jetliner-style oval windows, and even light fittings suggestive of the leading edge of a plane wing. Grimshaw's wave roof form at Zurich will be one of the biggest and most impressive of all, intended to become as much a symbol of the city as the Eiffel Tower in Paris.

CANOPIES

Increasingly, terminal roofs oversail glass walls to provide shade, with many extended even further to become canopies over the drop-off point. Foster incorporated this feature in his designs for Stansted and Chek Lap Kok, where the arched roofs curve forward like so many peaked caps. Their sheer scale makes them the dominant feature of the building. It is strange, nonetheless, how a canopy rarely covers more than the pavement or first few feet of roadway – the more so as many airports have more than one drop-off lane.

The risk of being drenched in a sudden downpour while unloading the luggage is evident in many airports, particularly as canopies are often set high and offer little protection against slanting or driving rain. One major exception is at Munich Airport, where the drop-off points – positioned on loops off the approach road – are beneath canopies that provide protection for all passengers wherever a car or coach may be positioned.

FORESTS

Giant roofs, especially those that appear to float on walls of glass, need internal support. Enter the tree form pioneered by Sir Norman Foster at London Stansted and Meinhard von Gerkan at Hamburg. Foster's 'trees', branching out to support huge roof panels have been the inspiration for numerous subsequent terminals. Von Gerkan's forms, reaching up to support long arching roof trusses, are no less impressive. At Stuttgart, von Gerkan develops the steel tree a stage further: four arms each branch into three and then again into four, like sticks of cow parsley, though the scale is that of a forest tree.

At Chek Lap Kok, Foster supports the roof on columns of almost pencil-thin proportions, while for sheer engineering virtuosity Barcelona's international terminal makes a powerful impression with just four columns – set far from the glass outside walls – supporting a roof measuring 130 by 80 metres.

COLOUR AND TEXTURE

Norman Foster's athletic high-tech designs and smart palette of greys have been imitated all over the world. He believes that in architecture, as in nature, colour should serve a purpose, and prefers to reserve colour for signs and other elements that need to attract the eye for functional reasons. Yet air travel would be less interesting if grey became an almost universal livery. For this reason, Munich Airport makes a radiant change, the equivalent of donning an all white suit in the tropics. Here is an airport in the mould of Richard Meier's work, or, more directly, one that takes its inspiration from the white-walled Baroque churches which are such a feature of the Bavarian landscape. Tropical white dominates, too, at Paul Andreu's elegant airport at Pointe-à-Pitre, Guadaloupe. Moneo's interiors at San Pablo Airport, Seville, set cool white against deep marine blue. White-tented roofs, echoing snow-capped peaks, give Denver one of the most romantic silhouettes of any airport terminal. And at Doha, in the starkly different desert environment, Fentress Bradburn introduces granite floors inspired by traditional Qatari patterns – with red for the sand, white for buildings, and blue-grey for the waters of the Gulf. Where white stone is used in arrivals, red is used in the corresponding position in departures.

Colour can be introduced in a variety of ways. In Frankfurt's Terminal 2, huge hanging advertising banners enliven an otherwise grey interior. A palette of colours can also be integrated through materials. At Oslo's Gardermoen there is an abundance of warm natural wood, oak and maple as well as cooler-toned marble. Kisho Kurokawa uses slatted wood at Kuala Lumpur on the underside of his billowing vaults, and at Chek Lap Kok the highly polished marble is so reflective that it appears coated with a film of water by a photographer determined to achieve stunning reflections.

AIRPORTS AS ART GALLERIES

Conscious of the tedium of long waits between flights, an increasing number of airports are commissioning and displaying large works of art – not just the murals or reliefs common in the early days of flying, but a whole range of specially designed three-dimensional artefacts, sculptures and fittings. Art has been commissioned on a grand scale at Denver Airport; not fine art, such as you might find in a museum, but a whole range of innovative works that will intrigue passengers of any

age: paper planes, musical chimes and a kinetic light sculpture consisting of 5,280 metal propellers that whizz into motion as the people mover train rushes through the tunnel.

AVIATION HISTORY ON DISPLAY

Airports could utilise their own history to a greater effect, exploring the aircraft and airlines that have used their facilities, and the way they have grown and changed. One star attraction along these lines is the Flughafen Modell (airport model) next to Terminal 1b at Hamburg. This is air travel's answer to a large-scale model train layout, or indeed to one of the numerous Legoland models involving moving planes and vehicles. The difference here is that the model planes actually take off and land by night: runways and taxiways are illuminated and all the different parts of the airport are explained in turn – fire service, fuel farm, cargo and maintenance. This exhibit is run by a group of enthusiasts who made the model and keep it up to date.

For all the new terminals featured in this book, elaborate and handsome models are likely to have been made, often showing elements that are planned for the future. These constitute an archive with considerable public appeal as well as future historical interest.

SHOPPING, EATING AND DRINKING

For years, airports were largely state or municipal enterprises, underwritten by the public purse and funded by landing fees and the occasional duty-free shop. One of the great exceptions was Brussels, an airport of no architectural grace but one packed with shops and bars selling every variety of chocolate and beer. Then came Pittsburgh, where the British Airports Authority won the contract to manage the terminal so pioneering a radical new approach to airport shopping. Hong Kong has now followed with what is claimed to be the largest congregation of airport shops in the world, bristling with names like Cartier, Gucci, Harrods and Calvin Klein.

In Europe, by far the most elegant airport shopping mall is the Ramblas at Barcelona Airport, designed by the Taller de Arquitectura. One kilometre in length, with moving walkways to speed the journey if desired, the mall is lined with smart freestanding kiosks containing shops and cafes. These clean-lined and stylishly finished kiosks are far more attractive than the usual row of shopfronts set around the perimeter of a departure

Foster & Partners, Chek Lap Kok Airport, Hong Kong

John Pawson, Cathay Pacific Lounges at Chek Lap Kok

concourse or shopping area. They have the appeal of kiosks along Barcelona's original Ramblas or the new kiosks along the Champs Elysées.

It is evident from the success of these shopping malls that airport passengers provide a discerning and ready market, not just for bottles of whisky, cigarettes, perfume, expensive watches and cameras, but for local food and wine, local crafts and clothes, and good books. The abolition of duty-free goods is presented as a loss to the air traveller but in many cases duty-free prices are hardly lower than those which the careful buyer can find in local shops. Removing this option may result in the provision of a better choice of goods, admitting a wider range of enterprising shops rather than the high mark-up selection that is typical of duty free. One of the best is the cheese shop at Terminal 1, Charles de Gaulle, which does a thriving trade in unusual but reasonably priced cheese in prime condition.

A colourful example is the new satellite terminal at Las Vegas, which comes with themed shopping gallerias inspired by the city's famous Strip and hotel and casino shows, by Area 51 and its associations with aliens, and by the desert. Neon lights and signs rival the city's own illuminations.

Scandinavian Service Partner (SSP) developed a new catering concept for airports at Oslo–Fornebu, with a wider range of small outlets offering both national and international specialities – a mix of in-house brands and local and international chains. The company believes that the right balance helps airports to convey individuality. On offer were sausages at Frank's Deli, seafood at Salmon House, coffee at Kaffehuset 1796 and waffles in the Vaffelhuset, as well as Burger King, Pizza Hut and Upper Crust. Such outlets operate with restricted space for food preparation and have minimal staff requirements.

RINGING THE WORLD

In spite of the proliferation of mobile phones, there is a strong demand for payphones at airports. While they are potentially part of a terminal's street furniture, people making telephone calls at airports appreciate some space, privacy and quiet. One neat solution is provided at Stuttgart, where generous-sized Perspex globes contain ledges large enough to open a briefcase or to set out papers. The globe shuts out external noise (especially loudspeaker announcements) and simultaneously keeps conversations more private. At Chek Lap Kok, Cathay Pacific has sponsored the introduction of a new generation of touch-screen phones.

The new terminal at Washington National Airport, which opened in July 1997, has two types of telephone: wall-mounted phones and sit-down phones in the holdrooms or departure gate areas. The latter are equipped with modem connections for laptop computers, providing passengers with a facility usually found only in airport lounges.

AIRLINE LOUNGES

Airport lounges have come to be an expected perk of the business traveller, offering drinks, snacks, privacy and extra comforts. They are often the work of interior designers, but all too many are more cramped than the seating areas in the public concourses. They can also be places where people talk in self-conscious, hushed tones and seem far from relaxed. For these reasons, airlines are now turning to architects to create spaces with an individual character, and placing a new emphasis on spaciousness, light and high-quality materials.

Nowhere are the results more spectacular than in the Cathay Pacific lounges designed by the British architect John Pawson at Chek Lap Kok. Cathay Pacific has taken

John Pawson, Cathay Pacific Lounges at Chek Lap Kok

Von Gerkan • Marg & Partner, Hamburg Airport

2,800 square metres at balcony level, overlooking one of the main arms of the giant public departure concourse. First class passengers can enter discreetly via a secret short cut from the check-in area and emerge beside an indoor canal which runs through the lounge. On one side there is a fully equipped spa where passengers can book a spacious cabana, consisting of a bathroom and private terrace overlooking the water. The relaxed environment makes use of sandstone walls and mahogany benches. Washbasins are solid blocks of Impala marble, while the 1.8-metre-long enamel bathtubs are designed for two.

The lounge will be operated by Hong Kong's fabled Peninsula Hotel. Guests who wish to sleep after take-off can enjoy a sumptuous buffet before departure, and perhaps ultimately, a fully fledged restaurant. There is also a well-stocked news stand and a library. John Pawson explains, 'I wanted to offer everyone personal living space, with a desk, computer, an armchair and a stool, so two people could study the screen together'.

Pawson's business-class lounge is designed to be as convivial as the best hotel. A long bar takes spectacular advantage of the floor-to-ceiling glass walls of Sir Norman Foster's terminal, affording panoramic views of taxiing planes and the hills beyond.

Everywhere the emphasis is on beautiful materials and finishes – straight-grained Japanese oak, American walnut, real leather and metre-square granite floor paving stones, cut so smoothly that no mortar is needed. In line with Pawson's belief that the ultimate crime is for a light to shine directly in your eye, all light sources are concealed, many built into the furniture.

The chairs have been selected to create a gallery of classic twentieth-century furniture design, consisting of one famous chair after another, all still in production.

CARPARKING

Self-evidently, the major landmark buildings in any airport should be the terminal(s). In recent years the sheer demand for parking close to check-in has led to the crowding of handsomely designed terminals by multi-storey car parks. If carparking is to be conveniently close to departures and arrivals it must be in front, beside or beneath the terminal. The Richard Rogers Partnership has created a tiered car park for the new Terminal 5 at London Heathrow in order to leave a clear view of the tall elevated departure level. At Munich, car parks ranged in front of the very long terminal are sunken. Elsewhere in Germany, notably at Stuttgart and Hamburg, the car parks have been designed as features in themselves, quite distinctive in form, materials and colour from the terminal. Circular ascent ramps are made into striking towers at Stuttgart, while another drum-shaped car park to the left of the terminal cleverly ranges the bonnets of every car around the perimeter. Since many cars are exhibits in themselves, this is an attractive option. The Farrell Transportation building at Inchon, Seoul, contains four levels of carparking below ground.

LANDSCAPING

Airports are essentially expanses of tarmac, but most incorporate large areas of grass between the runways and taxiways, and some of the most attractive are surrounded by lush vegetation. There are numerous airports in Africa that are enclosed completely by plantations of palm trees or thick forest. At Jakarta Airport in Indonesia, Paul Andreu has led the way not only in planting lush vegetation but by allowing passengers to walk outside along shaded terraces overlooking gardens. Similarly, at Bangkok's new airport, scheduled for completion in 2004, Murphy/Jahn plans extensive displays of flowering trees and topiary along the approaches, as well as large gardens under a vast oversailing canopy roof. These will be laid out by a local landscape designer and are intended to recall a Thai myth of forest spirits. At Kuala Lumpur Airport, which opened in 1998, the Japanese architect Kisho Kurokawa determined that the first sight arriving passengers should be confronted with was a rainforest vista. A lush, well-watered grove of trees is therefore placed at the centre of his new arrivals satellite.

One of the complaints about air travel is the way that it eliminates local character, producing a bland internationalism whereby any airport could be in any country. Vegetation, even more than art or heritage, gives an immediate stamp to a place, and usually by its very nature an exotic even romantic one – pine trees in winter can be just as appealing as palms.

As airports become ever busier, they are surrounded by increasing numbers of buildings – car parks, cargo depots, catering facilities, maintenance hangars, fuel farms, hotels, airport and airline offices – and well-maintained landscaping and planting can add an immensely calming effect.

One of the best examples of effective landscaping is at Munich's new airport. Here extensive, immaculately kept lawns along the approach roads create the impression of arriving at a grand hotel rather than at a crowded travel interchange. Regular lines of trees provide shade and car parks are skilfully shielded behind great banks of shrubs and ground cover. At Madrid's new terminal, where there will be extremes of summer heat and winter cold, the Richard Rogers Partnership intends to plant hardy vegetation which will emphasise the rich-toned local earth.

CHECK-IN

First impressions are always important. In every airport a lasting impression is created by the speed or slowness of its check-in procedures. Ever larger planes, particularly on intercontinental routes, can cause long queues to build up, blocking the path of other passengers. Terminals with check-in counters on islands or piers can be prone to this. So, equally, can an airport with a single long bank of check-in counters opposite the doors, particularly if the concourse is narrow and tailbacks block other passengers – and their trolleys – trying to cross the hall. Such problems are most likely

to arise with wide-bodied planes carrying a full payload or when computers break down as passengers are checking in.

An increasing number of airports are seeking to cope with this by utilising a flexible system of check-in counters. Instead of individual counters being assigned to airlines on a permanent basis, with permanent signs proclaiming their territory, check-in positions are assigned as required, with airline logos flashing up on screens behind or above the check-in counters. This opens up the possibility of increasing the number of check-in positions where a flight is heavily booked and will assist in reducing frustrating queuing times for harassed passengers.

Increasingly, airlines are using self-ticketing and self check-in facilities with the aid of ticket machines. This system is usually aimed at passengers travelling with hand baggage only – passengers with heavier baggage will still need to have it tagged and checked in.

An alternative that is developing in America, for example at Chicago, is the curb-side baggage check-in, where bags are tagged and taken immediately from the passenger, as at a busy city hotel. This reduces the need for passengers to manhandle heavy baggage on and off trolleys.

At Chek Lap Kok, Cathay Pacific has introduced a new counter-free form of check-in for first-class passengers, it consists of a series of island stands with computer screens displaying information. This is akin to open-plan banking or registration at grand hotels, where customers approach a table rather than a counter, where they can be seated and command the full attention of a member of staff.

BAGGAGE HANDLING AND SECURITY

Baggage-handling systems represent a major element of the cost of any new terminal. A whole floor level beneath arrivals and departures is likely to be assigned for this purpose. Being a secure area, it will be unseen by passengers and even unmarked on plans. Airport managers and airlines have strong views on baggage systems: some believe in maximum automation and computerisation and are keen to take advantage of the latest innovations, while others mistrust all but the most tried and tested systems and prefer porters and trolleys.

From check-in to aircraft, baggage handling can now be totally automated. Expensive outbound baggage

sorting and handling rooms can be eliminated. The system can be reversed for inbound bags, which can be directed automatically to the appropriate baggage-claim carousel or to a specified transfer aircraft. Traditional tugs and carts, nonetheless, continue to be used at many airports because they are less subject to mechanical breakdowns. The disadvantage is that they add to congestion on the airside roads and aprons, and allow human error to lead to lost and misdirected baggage.

By contrast the new automated baggage systems are equipped with electric-eye checking stations so that if a piece of baggage goes missing its progress through the airport (and possible departure on the wrong plane) has been recorded stage by stage and can be checked against the baggage counterfoil given to the passenger at check-in.

Pittsburgh's $33 million automated baggage system uses lasers, computers and fibre-optics networks to direct baggage from aeroplanes to baggage carousels a mile away. Coded tags are read by 360-degree laser scanners and sent on conveyor belts along underground tunnels to their destination. Additional scanners along the route verify that the case is on course, and provide an instant record of the last time each piece passed a check-point. This system is claimed as having a near-perfect rating.

It is standard procedure to search or to screen hand luggage at all airports, using X-rays and metal detectors. Now an increasing number of airports are seeking to check all passenger baggage destined for the aircraft hold, rather than just a random sample as has long been standard practice. In November 1996, Manchester Airport became the first airport in the UK to screen all international hold baggage. Ten new CTX 5000 screen units, acting as both 'nose and eye' to provide advanced detection powers, were installed at a cost of £14 million with a cost per passenger bag of 44 pence. Once operational, this was the only fully certified explosives detection system as recommended by the US Federal Aviation Administration.

ABOVE: Leo A Daly and Tate & Snyder, McCarran Airport, Las Vegas; CENTRE: Washington Dulles Airport; BELOW: Kisho Kurokawa Architects, Kuala Lumpur Airport

X-ray screens are, in turn, dependent on the alertness of their operators. Michael Cantor, a psychologist who specialises in researching how people find things – from cereal in the supermarket to golf balls in the rough – has tested security screening staff. Security screeners in Europe scored an average 9.5 out of 18, and those at US airports 3.5 points. This compared with a college student rating of 12 out of 18. Cantor's worrying findings fuelled a debate on whether screening was a minimum-wage job, attracting people without the necessary cognitive skills.

Some authorities advocate the use of dogs, but they like humans can quickly become bored. Moreover, the dog requires an officer who also needs to be trained (and tested and retrained), and the dog can only work for about twenty minutes before boredom sets in. A bomb-sniffing dog may cost around $8,500 to train compared with a $1 million X-ray machine and the ability of the machine to detect plastic explosives at speed is disputed.

FIRE

Major air terminals around the world are high-specification buildings, often substantially constructed of non-combustible materials. Nonetheless, fires can break out despite the most exhaustive fire precautions and fire detection systems. As air terminals are places where the public gathers in large numbers, this is a subject which has to be kept under constant review.

The dangers are illustrated by the terrible fire at Dusseldorf, which broke out in a flower shop and swept through the arrivals hall of the city's airport late on the afternoon of 11 April 1996. The story is related graphically by Neil Wallington in *Firefighting A Pictorial History* (1997). At the time, the hall was packed with 2,500 travellers and staff. Sixteen people lost their lives and over 100 were injured. Thick smoke rising from burning plastic furnishings quickly filled the hall, asphyxiating people trapped in shops and lavatories. Nine of the dead were trapped in lifts.

The fire is believed to have been started by sparks from a workman's power tool. It took hold in a false ceiling and spread rapidly through ventilation and service ducting to affect remote parts of the terminal, including the departure halls, with terrifying speed. The airport approach roads were closed, causing huge traffic jams and delaying the assistance of extra fire engines from the city and beyond.

This was a modern building with numerous fire exits but despite repeated public announcements to evacuate the area many people were bewildered and disoriented. Paramedics and doctors provided aid to unconscious victims as they were dragged out into the open by firemen using breathing apparatus. However the search for victims was hampered by the collapse of ceilings and walls which brought down pipework and ducting.

A very different fire strategy has been developed for Foster & Partners' new terminal at Chek Lap Kok, where the whole terminal interior is effectively one single fire compartment, unbroken by internal subdivisions. Fire prevention and containment strategy is based on avoiding combustible materials in construction. Moreover, where there is a source of fire risk, for example a shop or kitchen, the establishment is equipped with sprinklers and roller shutters. As soon as the fire alarm is triggered, the air-conditioning is switched off, and powerful fans extract air and any smoke or fumes through the roof.

AIRPORTS AS NEIGHBOURS

While air travel may be inexorably on the increase, aircraft, whether landing or taking off, cause considerable annoyance and sometimes misery to people living under the flightpath. Of the great conurbations, London is one of the worst affected. Vast swathes of south-west London (including what for centuries were considered the most idyllic reaches of the River Thames, around Richmond and Twickenham, as well as Windsor Castle and its great park) are subject almost every minute of the day to the drone or roar of low-flying aircraft. Indeed, it often seems that local residents are powerless in the face of economic imperatives, whatever sops are offered in the way of public inquiries or restrictions on night flying. Free double-glazing may help indoors but not when people wish to sleep with the window open (a fairly elementary freedom) or to enjoy their gardens.

It is important to realise that noise pollution from airports is a worldwide problem, and that environmental groups, particularly in North America, are making headway in gaining real reductions in noise and intrusiveness. Clearly, it is universally desirable that manufacturers produce aircraft and aircraft engines that generate less and less noise. The sheer number of people affected by the growing volume of air traffic around the world should force the issue higher up the agenda of aircraft manufacturers, airport authorities, airlines and city and national governments.

AIRPORTS FOR THE FUTURE

Today's architects exert themselves to produce buildings that are simple to use and negotiate, spacious, calming and pleasant to spend time in. Hence the increasing emphasis on daylight, airiness, and lofty proportions. But there is an alternative view, trenchantly expressed by the columnist Simon Jenkins in London's *Evening Standard* on 26 September 1997:

> I love some airports, especially Heathrow. It is London's seething, smelly, down-at-heel gateway. It is Old Docklands reincarnated, a shambles teaming with people and sin. Each time I approach the access tunnel I expect to see the heads of thieving baggage handlers impaled on the spike of the tacky Concorde model . . . Heathrow doubles as Butlin's and Britain's Ellis Island. For the streetwise it offers the fastest dash from car to plane in Europe. For the ingenue, it is a Third World Waterfront, swarming with lascars, bureaucrats and cutpurses.

Jenkins asserts that 'Modern airports were built by Governments, largely for prestige'. Contrast, he says, the areas where customer choice is sovereign:

> Look at the club lounges, bars, cafes and shopfronts of modern airports. Gatwick's shopping mall is now called a village . . .Passengers at Heathrow search for leather, wood panelling, table lamps, 'pubs' and private lounges.

The airports in this book represent the architectural expression of a decade in which patronage has begun to move from government to the commercial sector. Customer needs and desires are becoming more of a priority. A new dimension in airport design was put forward by Peter Hodgkinson of the Taller de Arquitectura for a new airport to serve the booming leisure sector on Tenerife. Large numbers of tourists come to the Canaries on package holidays, and hotels are keen to release departing guests before new ones arrive, leaving as much time as possible to prepare rooms. As a result, some passengers can be faced with very long waits.

The new terminal planned by Peter Hodgkinson was designed to have the ambience and facilities of a country club as much as a terminal, with opportunities for passengers to swim, sunbathe and play games. While this project is on hold, across the globe Singapore's Changi has already pioneered this concept in relaxation. Many connecting passengers choose Singapore as a stopover or hub because it offers the use of a swimming pool.

At Changi there is a Transit Hotel Complex, with fifty furnished rooms, sauna and shower rooms, a fitness centre and a rooftop swimming pool and jacuzzi, a poolside bar and a putting green for golfers. Other facilities include a business centre, nursery, karaoke lounge and hairdressing salon. According to *Passenger Terminal World* (January–March 1997), Changi is the first airport in the world to have a twenty-four-hour Internet centre. This service is located in the departure transit lounge of Terminal 2, providing both information (a homepage describes Singapore's history, people and festivals) and entertainment. It allows the business passenger to make full use of his or her time and has the added advantage of providing the most up-to-date play technology. Travellers can send, retrieve, download and print e-mail, scan documents or take digital photographs to attach to outgoing e-mail. They can charge-up notebook computers, surf the World Wide Web, and communicate with other Internet users.

The 1990s may come to represent a high watermark in terminal building. There is already a trend towards pre-airport check-in, usually at city railway stations. If this spreads it will lead to a reduction in the size of airport check-in halls – at present a dominant feature occupying the prime position at most airports. Over the last decade, more and more space has been taken up by baggage-handling facilities, in many cases at least a whole floor of a very large building.

Thought is being given now to alternatives: for example, home baggage collection, several hours before a flight departs, relieving passengers of the need to struggle to the airport with their baggage. If such a trend was to develop, much baggage sorting could take place in a building quite separate from the terminal, even away from the airport altogether. Of course, there will always be a demand for baggage check-in at the airport, but faced with the burgeoning costs of space and security, alternatives will continue to be investigated.

The dominant trend apparent in this book is that bigger is better. It cannot be long before the cry of small is beautiful returns dramatically to terminal design.

NEW BANGKOK INTERNATIONAL AIRPORT
Thailand

Nong Ngu Hao, which translates as 'cobra swamp', is one of the new generation of megaterminals planned for a site east of Bangkok. Its flat farmland position ensures that the new terminal will be a landmark for miles around. First the land must be drained: following a method proposed by a Dutch company, a poulder or dam will be constructed round the site and water pumped out. Although the process is incessant, it has for centuries been used successfully by the Dutch for draining low-lying land.

The competition to design New Bangkok was launched in 1996 and on-site work scheduled to begin in 1998. Construction of the terminal is forecast to start in 1999, with opening planned for 2004. The stated intention of the client, the Airports Authority of Thailand, is to construct the terminal incrementally, with the first phase providing some fifty gates and 500,000 square metres of terminal facilities.

The new approach road from Bangkok will be constructed above ground level as it nears the terminal, drawing in at a raised arrivals level. A spur will climb to departures level, situated three levels above arrivals. Convenient land access will be completed by a rail link in Phase II of the project, for which no construction date has yet been fixed.

The overall plan is a giant H with the crossbar extruded on either side, reminiscent of a rugby goal. Murphy/Jahn points out that this concept sets passenger circulation over aircraft circulation and states that it is the most compact of the terminal forms studied.

The grand gesture of the scheme is a large roof trellis, raised high and shading a series of functionally separate structures and spaces beneath. This conveys a powerful and consistent image, while allowing great flexibility for future growth and change. Louvres shade the structures

OPPOSITE AND ABOVE: Model views

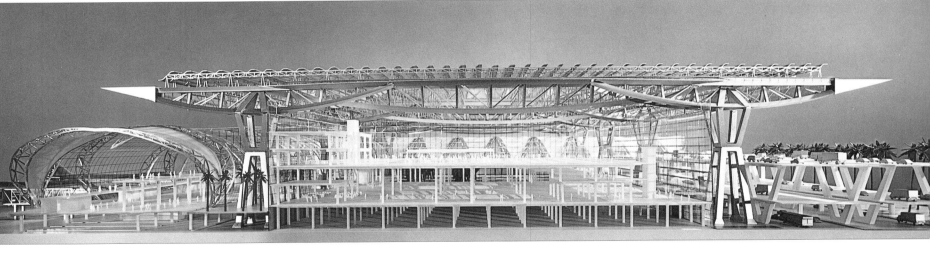

below from direct sunlight, thereby reducing energy demands.

The ticketing area is rectangular with the structure suspended from the trellis girders. As a result of the overall roof form, the terminal can be faced entirely in well-shaded glass, allowing clear views out in all directions. The interiors will be used for displays of local art. Brian O'Connor, the project architect, says, 'We consider the building as a backdrop. What will make it a Thai airport is the clothes people wear.'

To this end, the interior is conceived partly as theatre, where the maximum number of people are on view as they move through the terminal. From the check-in area, departing passengers progress down one level to the airside centre where there are shops and cafes, and then descend to the departure concourses where the gates and holdrooms are situated. All movement will be visible from bridges and balconies above.

The concourses are tubular tunnels that look almost like giant Chinese lanterns expanding concertina-fashion over metal girders. These are wrapped in alternating bands of white and transparent roofing, with the festive look of an ultra-modern marquee.

Empty spaces under the canopy are to be landscaped as gardens and courtyards. As O'Connor explains:

> The overall roof lets the sun through in places. The Thais working on the gardens have designed them around a Thai myth of forest spirits which will be immediately recognisable to their fellow countrymen.

However, it will be too hot, he says, for passengers to sit or walk in the gardens. The idea is taken from Thai architecture, where buildings have strong overhangs and the gardens tend to be designed to look at, not sit in.

Extensive planting is planned along the approaches to the airport, incorporating an abundance of flowering trees and topiary. This will shield the ground level of the terminal which is used for services. 'It will be typically Thai, very colourful and very tailored', insists O'Connor.

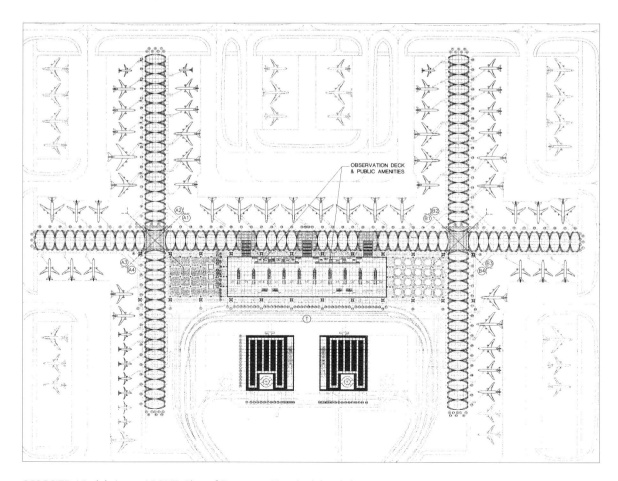

OPPOSITE: Model views; ABOVE: Plan of Passenger Terminal, level six

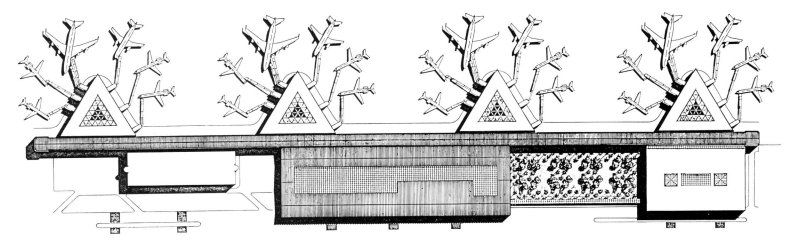

Roof plan

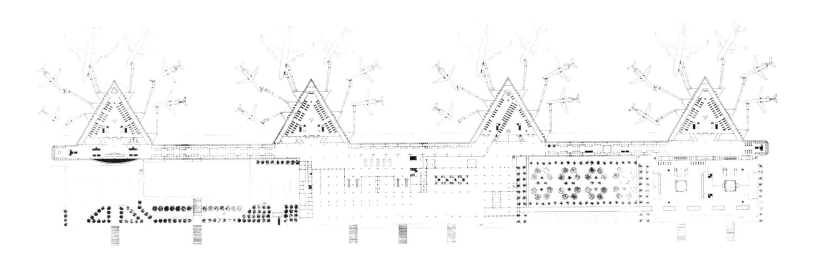

First floor plan

RICARDO BOFILL, TALLER DE ARQUITECTURA
BARCELONA AIRPORT, NEW TERMINAL
Spain

Ricardo Bofill's giant Classicism of the 1980s is the very antithesis of the minimalist Modernism that is now dominant in Spanish architecture and in Europe as a whole. The Taller de Arquitectura's extensions to Barcelona Airport are certainly monumental and incorporate classical columns, but above all they are light, airy, open and transparent. The scale may be colossal but it is the sense of space not mass which creates the most striking impression.

The additions consist of a new international terminal which connects to a kilometre-long concourse used by both departing and arriving passengers. This also serves the centrally placed European terminal and a shuttle terminal at the far end with half-hourly flights to Madrid and frequent flights to the Balearic Islands.

Peter Hodgkinson, the partner in charge, explains:

> The whole concept is based on a ground-level building with arriving and departing passengers leaving and entering at street level. Behind the check-in desks, baggage is also handled at ground level so no underground floors or tunnels are necessary.

This layout also avoids the need for expensive overhead roadways serving an upper departures level.

The departures hall of the international terminal is an engineering *tour de force*. The huge roof is supported by just four freestanding concrete columns set 90 metres apart in one direction and 40 metres in the other. These carry two master and two secondary trusses, which extend to cover a space measuring 130 by 80 metres. The trusses are 9 metres high and of zig-zag construction like railway bridges.

The engineers were Ove Arup and Partners. The company's John Thornton explains:

> The technical solution is very simple. Large solid concrete columns support a system of tied rafters – like an A-frame. The simplicity of it all allows fantastic clarity and lightness.

The size of the space is emphasised by the unbroken walls of glass. The glass forms a double skin ventilated at the top in order to provide protective insulation in hot weather as well as in Barcelona's few cold winter spells. The same double skin continues along the high level concourse serving the departure gates. The glass panels measure 2.50 by 1.25 metres and are held in place by steel fingers attached to fins inserted between the two layers of glass.

The lower panels are of clear glass allowing passengers an unrestricted view of the aircraft. Above, the glass becomes increasingly dark towards the top. Smoked glass is used to combat the effects of the sun. According to Hodgkinson there are no problems with condensation and on the airside the glass has excellent acoustic values, breaking up 'the decibel attack from the aircraft outside'. Externally the glass walls run uniformly around the terminal and to mark the entrance the architects introduced a gentle bow in the facade.

They also decided to give the main hall of the international terminal a distinctive character by introducing palm trees. Unfortunately, the leaves began to wilt and the airport authorities felt obliged to remove them in 1998. Peter Hodgkinson comments:

> We're furious. There is no problem with having palm trees indoors so long as they are ventilated; this can be done with the aid of a small motor. The airport authority simply failed to follow our instructions.

From the ground level check-in hall, passengers ascend via escalators and lifts to the departure concourse. There are also broad flights of steps, where passengers tend to sit and watch the throng below. 'It's like the Spanish Steps in Rome,' says Hodgkinson.

Hodgkinson designed the upper concourse as a version of Barcelona's famous Ramblas: a long street with a central promenade and numerous stalls, kiosks and places to sit. Shopping in airports often takes place in a self-contained area, separate from the walk to the departure gates. Here the two are merged, to the benefit of trade and the convenience of passengers who can shop until final boarding begins. Departure gates open off a series of triangular 'bastions', again clad in glass, each with ten gates – six connected with air-bridges and four linked with bus gates below to allow transfer to aircraft parked at remote stands. In these triangular waiting areas there is ample seating for passengers.

At regular intervals along the concourse there are moving walkways to speed passengers on their way. These are raised 30 centimetres above floor level. Hodgkinson explains:

> It is a British invention. As they're placed on the floor, rather than sunk into it, they can be moved as desired. You only have to make a small hole about the size of a table for the operating machinery.

The architects were also responsible for the design of the kiosks, which the airport chose to repeat for new shops or stalls.

The departures hall and concourse are paved in a sienna-pink marble from Almeria in southern Spain. Concrete surfaces are the beige colour of English Ham stone, false ceilings are egg-white and solid walls in the public areas are faced in off-white tiles. Stainless steel and aluminium are used for many details.

The concourse is shared by departing and arriving passengers. Its design also provides a welcome contrast to the numerous airports where arriving passengers descend straight to the bowels of the building where they queue at passport control and baggage claim in areas deprived of natural light. As if to complement the restrained and restful pastel tones of the construction materials, night-time light levels are lower than in many airports to avoid glare.

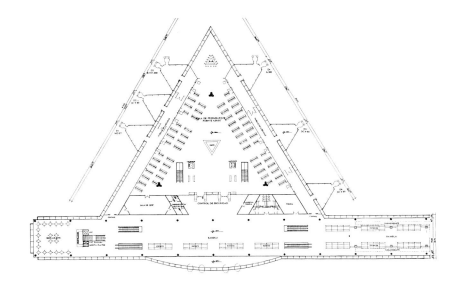

Domestic Terminal, first floor plan

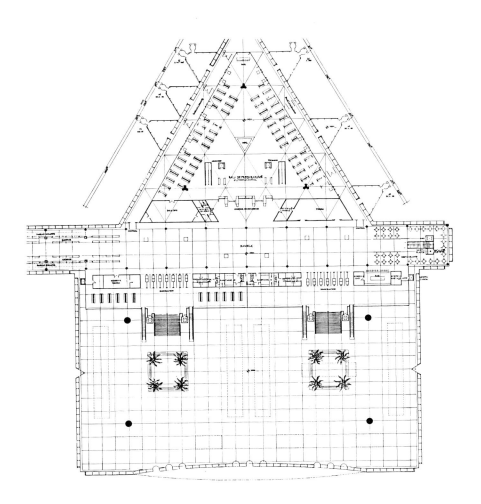

International Terminal, first floor plan

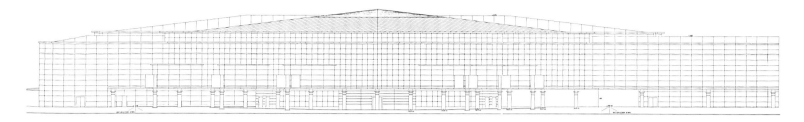

International Terminal, elevation

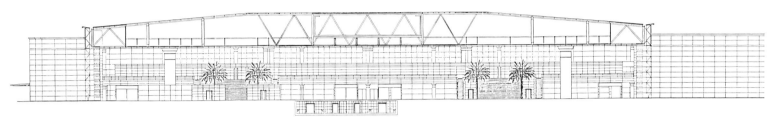

International Terminal, section

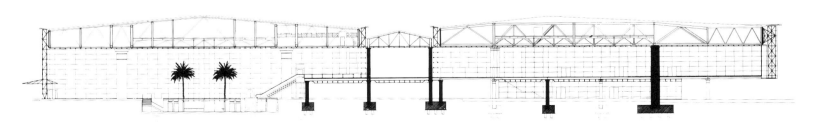

International Terminal, section

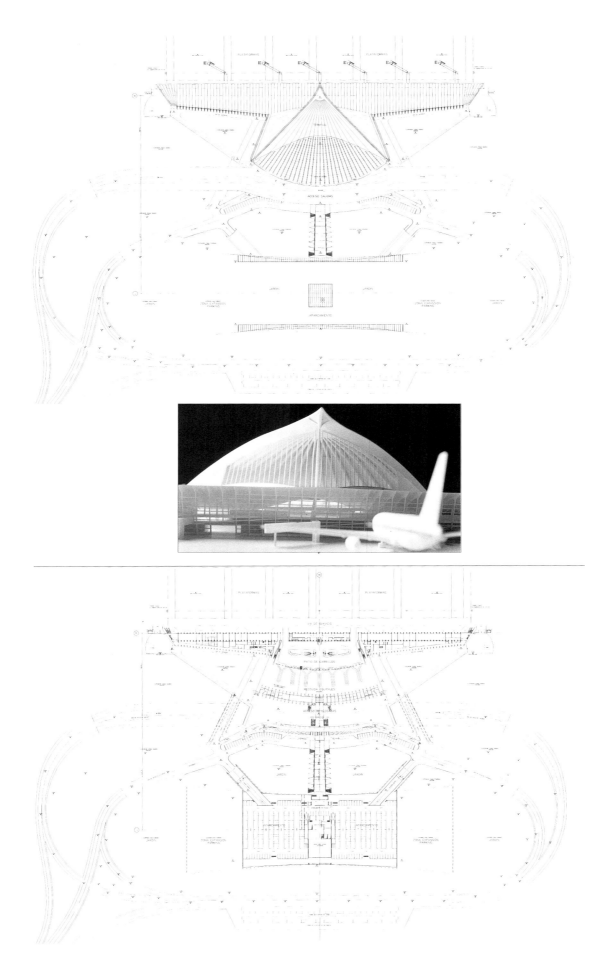

FROM ABOVE: Roof plan; model view; departures level plan

SANTIAGO CALATRAVA
SONDICA AIRPORT
Bilbao, Spain

Not since Eero Saarinen's famous TWA terminal in New York (1956–62) has an airport building been so expressive of the soaring grace and excitement of flight as Santiago Calatrava's new terminal for Bilbao, designed in 1990. Calatrava explains:

> It is very important how you arrive and how you leave. The terminal at Bilbao is a gate. I wish to create a strong image; hence the big roof. This is the fifth facade. It is still prominent as the airport is seen from the surrounding hills.

The new terminal has four levels, with an upper departures level, and a ground level arrivals hall. Departures lounges or holdrooms are located in two lateral wings, designed so they can be extended progressively to meet demand; eventually providing up to a maximum of fifty docking places. Calatrava's idea is to keep walking distances to planes at a minimum – 250 metres at the most.

The concourse is triangular in plan with a steel roof. As Calatrava relates, the north of Spain has a tradition of steel buildings and the most renowned companies are in Bilbao. His intention was to provide them with the opportunity to communicate their potential: 'The steel beams have a span of 120 metres – that's a lot for a beam.' The terminal is planned as a very low-budget building, using simple materials such as steel and concrete, which are exposed. There is no cladding.

The prominent structure of the roof is also designed to create order. As Calatrava explains, the interior of a terminal at pedestrian level can be very busy with numerous panels and signs. The lofty roof enables large areas of glass to be introduced, resulting in eighty per cent natural lighting. In contrast to the height of the departure hall, the waiting wings are lower.

Calatrava has also designed the newly constructed 42-metre-high control tower, located some 270 metres from the terminal. Rather than taper upwards, the tower grows in girth as it rises, culminating in a control deck affording the usual 360-degree visibility. Built of concrete and clad in aluminium, it is highly sculptural in form and cutaway to reveal the inner volume: an effect akin to an open-necked shirt sporting a dashing cravat.

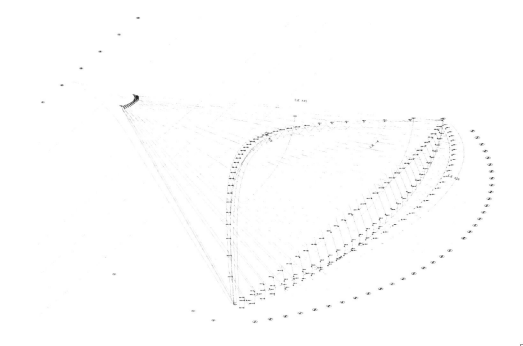

Axonometric of concourse

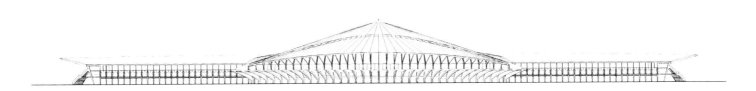

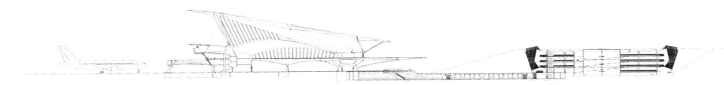

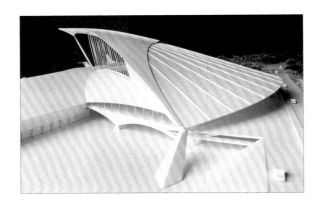

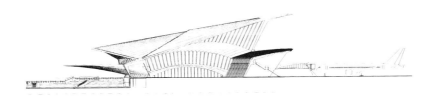

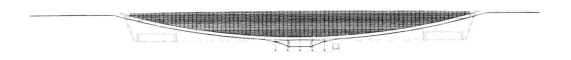

FROM ABOVE: North elevation; section; model detail; west elevation; section

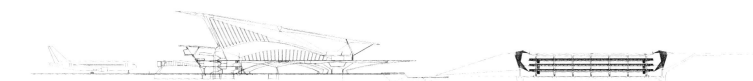

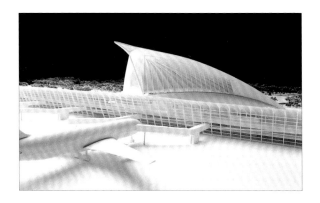

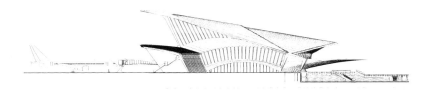

FROM ABOVE: South elevation; section; model detail; east elevation; section

LAURENT WILLOX

BRUSSELS NATIONAL AIRPORT, NEW TERMINAL

Zaventem, Belgium

In 1958, Brussels' original airport terminal was opened in Zaventem in time for the Brussels World Fair, with a capacity of six million passengers a year. In 1977, a new pier and departure concourse, known as the Satellite, were completed. Ten years later, the Brussels Airport Terminal Company (BATC) was formed, a venture owned jointly by the Belgian Airports and Airways Agency and a consortium of banks and institutions.

By 1990, annual passenger throughput had reached over eight million and work was started on a new terminal, next to the existing one, to meet the pressing need for expansion. This building, and Concourse B, opened in 1994, taking total airport capacity to twenty-one million passengers a year. By the end of the century, the airport is to be enlarged to handle an annual capacity of twenty-six million passengers. A new airport railway station beneath the terminal will also have opened by this time, providing direct access to the European rail network.

The new Concourse B has twenty-three gates, equipped with airbridges or jetways. Passengers travelling on commuter aircraft too small to use the airbridges have at their disposal six departure lounges on the ground level of Concourse B and eight at the Topaz terminal (opened in 1995), which is linked to the main building by underground travelators.

The old terminal was crowded and makeshift, but bustling and full of good shops. The new facility is contrastingly cool, sleek and spacious with floors of red Madagascar granite and special sound proofing to reduce noise levels. Public voice systems are confined to paging and special flight announcements, with the aim of creating an almost 'silent' airport. It is claimed to be the first terminal in Europe with a bar-code scanning system for baggage sorting.

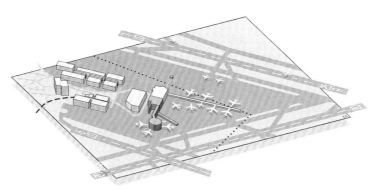

Axonometric of Concourse B and new terminal connected to existing satellite and south finger

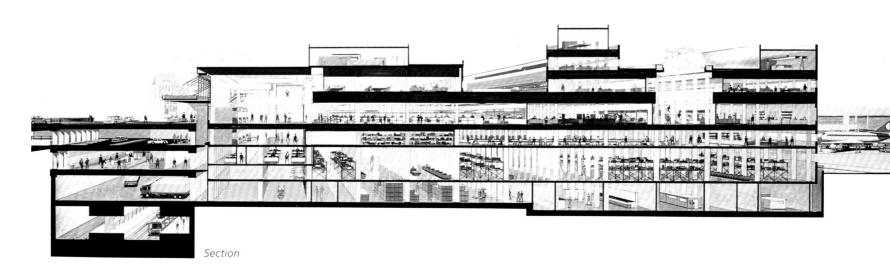

Section

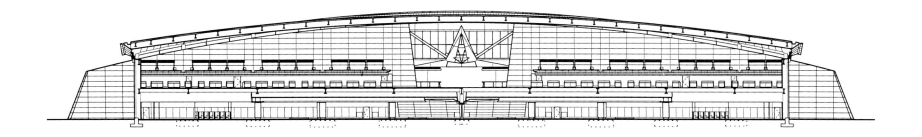

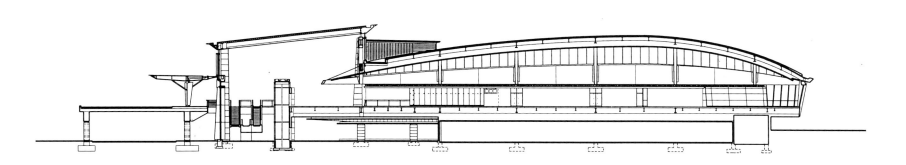

FROM ABOVE: Cross section; computer-generated perspectives; longitudinal section; OPPOSITE, FROM ABOVE: Plan of departures level; computer-generated perspective

KPF ARCHITECTS AND WNB+A
GREATER BUFFALO INTERNATIONAL AIRPORT

New York State, US

This $100 million terminal was built for the Niagara Frontier Transportation Authority and was completed in October 1997. A new fifteen-gate terminal replaces the existing east and west terminals, uniting all the airlines using the airport in one building.

The scheme consists of three major components: a departure hall, the departures and arrivals concourse and a public lounge and concessions area linking the two. There is ample provision for expansion, and a plan to build a hotel linked to the terminal by covered walks.

The design is intended to suggest aircraft technology, with the ends of the building lifting as in take-off. The main construction materials are glass, steel and metal cladding.

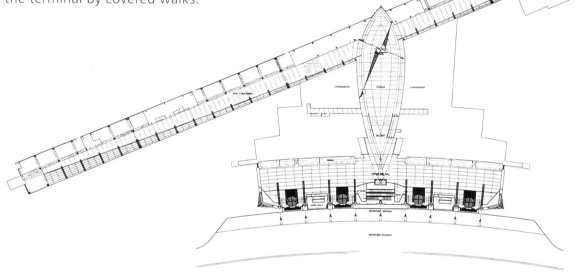

MURPHY/JAHN
O'HARE INTERNATIONAL AIRPORT, TERMINAL 1
Chicago, Illinois, US

United Airlines' new terminal illustrates utilitarian architecture on a grand scale: a broad underground avenue connects not one but two 'super-sheds' in the form of two parallel concourses. As one of several major projects to be undertaken at Chicago O'Hare, this structure replaces the former international Concourses B, C and D, as well as existing facilities for commuter and general aviation. Forty-two gates and some 111,500 square metres of new facilities are provided.

Previously, Y-shaped concourses had been prevalent at O'Hare. Here, two linear concourses eliminate dead-ends on the apron, reducing aircraft waiting time. Two-way taxiing is possible in the 250-metre gap between the concourses, and the whole perimeter of the island concourse is available as frontage for aircraft as they embark and disembark passengers.

The ticketing pavilion is adjacent to the upper roadway while baggage claim is at the lower level. The eye-catching bright red canopy along the drop-off point is shallow, not even reaching the edge of the pavement. However, there are curb-side baggage check-in facilities on either side of the vestibules, intended to cut down vehicle waiting times. The ticket hall, or ticketing pavilion, has an array of fifty-six flow-through ticket counters, where tickets can be bought and baggage checked in.

The new Concourse B is the long pier linking the departure gates in the main terminal. The engineering ethic comes even more strongly to the fore in this lofty atrium, which might almost have been assembled from a giant Meccano kit. Its dramatic 490-metre length is breathtaking, with a perspective of arches diminishing into the far distance. A break is introduced at each end, where the number of people approaching the gates diminishes. Monotony is avoided by variations in the colour and pattern of the glass, and by a wilful asymmetry which breaks up what could be a tunnel-like space inducing claustrophobia. The exhilarating effect of sunlight falling through windows on to a floor is exploited by extending the central band of glazing in each bay.

Approximately forty per cent of passengers depart from holdrooms along Concourse B; the remainder proceeds to escalators and then to moving walkways which speed the route through the 245-metre tunnel leading to the new Concourse C.

At airports around the world, architects and designers have experimented with ways of

enlivening long underground walkways. Here, a 'street' has been created that is as bright as any in Tokyo and effective in its apparent asymmetry. On one side is a continuous snaking wall (the kind known as a crinkle-crankle wall in eighteenth-century gardens) and a matching canopy. This is formed of back-lit panels in shades from all the colours of the spectrum, as in a paint chart; some of an amber richness, alternating with bursts of white glass in the canopy. The ceiling panels cast aqueous reflections on the walkways, brought to life by a wild tangle of spaghetti neon. Created by the artist Michael Hayden, this light sculpture is computer generated and the pattern of light pulses is never repetitive, synchronised with music by the composer William Craft.

Concourse D, the island pier at the end with twenty-six gates, will serve the majority of United Airlines' transfer passengers. Internally, it is laid out with a 15-metre-wide pedestrian walkway with moving pavements and 9-metre-deep hold-rooms on either side. The centre of Concourse C is deeper in plan, accommodating large 747 holdrooms, a major restaurant and UAL's Red Carpet Room. Arriving passengers walk back to the main terminal through the tunnel to the low-level baggage claim area. This fronts on to the lower level roadway, as well as linking to the underground garage and people mover system.

The nerve centre of the baggage handling system is located in the 27,870-square-metre underground bag room which extends beneath the apron between the two structures. Here, all outbound baggage is sorted by flight and automatically assembled for dispatch via tug and cart to the aircraft on the apron.

The underground baggage system is fed via conveyor from points all over the terminal — from bag checks at the upper level roadway, from flow through devices in the ticketing pavilion, from input stations (for on-line transfers), located along the baggage road at the back of the baggage claim area, and input stations at apron level of Concourses B and C. By contrast, inbound baggage is handled conventionally by tug and cart trains loaded from the hold of the arriving aircraft.

The structure consists of a steel frame supported on a foundation of concrete caissons and spread footings. Bay sizes vary from 9 by 36 metres to 9 by 8 metres. Floor systems comprise lightweight concrete fill on metal decks. The roof framing of the ticketing pavilion is a 'folded' truss system creating 36-metre spans across the hall allowing complete freedom of layout below.

The framing of the concourse vaults consists of rolled steel sections set at 9-metre intervals, with holes punched in to increase lightness and transparency. Steel purlins support the curtain walling. The steel arches are supported on 'bundled' columns in clusters of one to five according to the loading.

During the day, lighting is by natural means: each holdroom has skylighting, as has each line of roof in the ticketing pavilion, brightening interiors and reducing energy costs significantly. Combinations of opaque metal and clear and fritted glass control daylight in the concourses. Gull-wing light baffles are suspended beneath the linear skylights, filtering direct sunlight and redirecting it on to ceilings. At night, all artificial lighting is by indirect means, the gull-wings in the holdrooms and ticketing pavilion incorporating high-output fluorescent and metal halide fixtures directed on to ceilings.

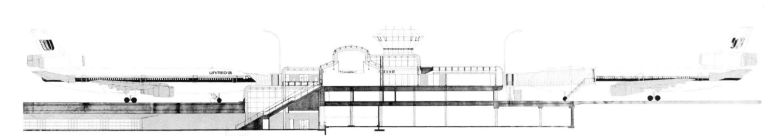

Section of Concourse C

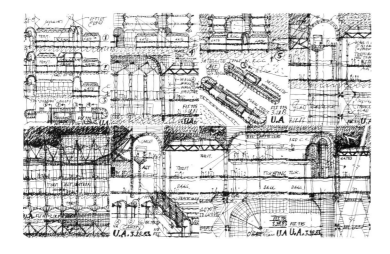

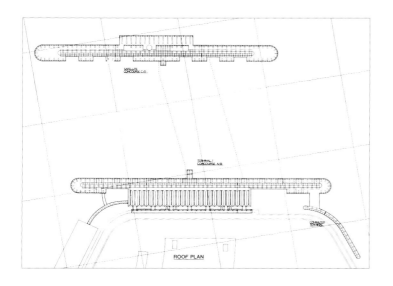

ROOF PLAN

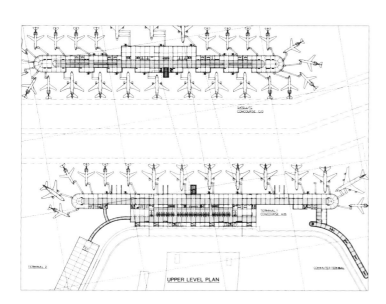

UPPER LEVEL PLAN

FROM ABOVE: Schematic drawings; roof plan; upper level plan

PERKINS & WILL
O'HARE INTERNATIONAL AIRPORT, TERMINAL 5
Chicago, Illinois, US

Completed in 1994, this awe-inspiring terminal (produced at a cost of $618 million) appears at first glance to be a masterpiece of simplicity: comprised of just two giant gentle arcs, one seen in silhouette, the other evident in plan. The shallow, immensely broad arch of the main elevation is in fact a graceful metaphor for the arc of flight.

The terminal's 1.1 million square feet represents a brilliant interweaving of functions, spaces and levels, that at once makes the most of its huge dimensions yet at the same time contrives to keep walking distances to reasonable length.

The triangular shape of the site was determined by existing taxiways to the south and west and the route of the automated rubber-tyre people mover, which links O'Hare's terminals with remote parking to the north and east.

The new terminal serves foreign flag departures and international arrivals for the entire airport, its twenty gates having sufficient capacity to accommodate the largest jumbos. Situated adjacent to the main road into the airport, the Perkins & Will terminal is the first structure visible to passing motorists, and acts as a beacon at night.

There are three primary levels. The upper level serves departing passengers, with ticketing, security checkpoints, shops, departure holdrooms, airline lounges and offices. The lower levels serve arrivals, with the Federal Inspection Service (FIS), capable of processing 4,000 passengers an hour, and the area for welcoming and meeting arrivals. A third intermediate (apron) level contains the people mover (ATS) station and airline support services such as baggage processing. A fourth level houses administrative and mechanical services and is located on a mezzanine above the main upper level.

The central feature of the scheme is the 250-metre-long vaulted steel and glass ticketing pavilion. The great roof, reminiscent of an aircraft hangar, is lit by continuous, narrow bands of skylights. Three external pavilions, with wedge-shaped glass roofs signal the presence of the people mover. Passengers walk from the drop-off point across bridges over the tracks into the ticketing hall.

Passengers then proceed along a galleria to a centrally placed concessions court. Curving departure corridors connect to rotundas at either end of the main terminal building. Extending outward from these rotundas are two concourses, one 370 metres long and the other 250 metres long. Numerous moving walkways, serving both arriving and departing passengers separately, speed passengers through the terminal. The architects

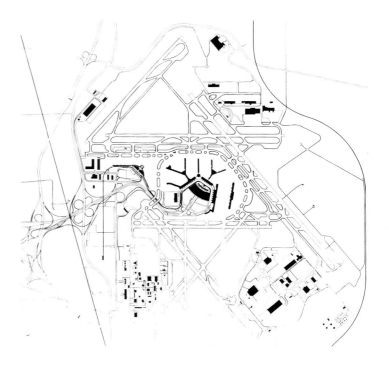

Site plan

have set out to maximise views, both landside and airside, to assist orientation and reduce dependence on signs. On the airside of the terminal, the central ramp control tower forms a prominent focal point from which travellers can readily gain their bearings.

At arrivals level, undulating wave roofs help create a greater sense of spaciousness. Ralph Johnson of Perkins & Will explains:

> In the arrivals hall, we were able to provide borrowed light from the stations of the people mover, while introducing skylights over immigration and baggage claim. There are very few terminals with good arrival spaces, because they tend to be at the lower levels.

The terminal is designed by a Chicago team consisting of two architectural practices: Perkins & Will, assisted by Heard & Associates, with

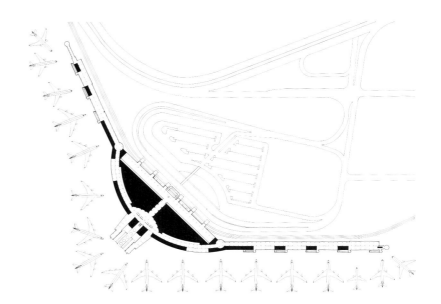

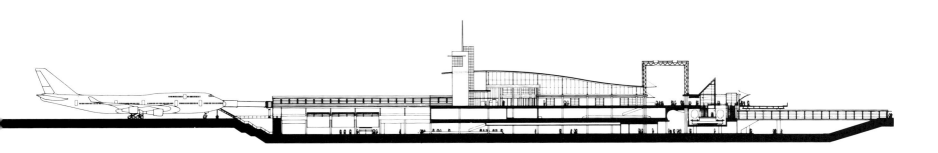

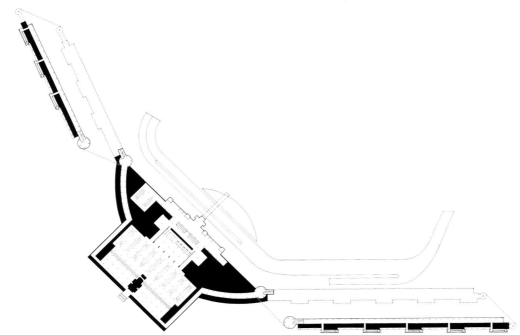

FROM ABOVE: Upper level plan; section; lower level plan

civil engineers Consoer, Townsend & Associates. The commission was received in 1986. Ralph Johnson (who designed the thirty-six storey Morton International Building in downtown Chicago) acted as design principal, with James Stevenson as managing principal and August Battaglia as a senior designer.

Previously, O'Hare Associates – a joint venture led by C F Murphy & Associates (which became Murphy/Jahn) – created project books for 140 separate schemes in the O'Hare Development Programme. This began in 1981, with James Stevenson as general manager until 1988.

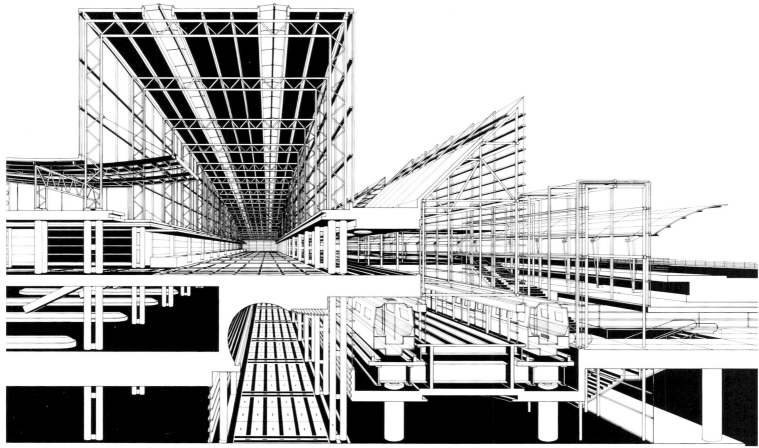

Sectional perspective

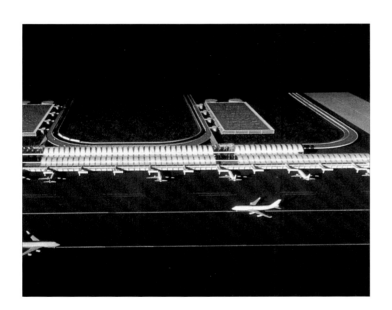

Computer-generated perspectives; OPPOSITE, L TO R: Computer-generated aerial view; simultaneous precision instrument approaches

TAMS
CHICAGO SOUTH SUBURBAN AIRPORT
Illinois, US

With an estimated construction cost of $4,900 million, this is one of the world's most ambitious new airport ventures. It is based on the premise that Chicago O'Hare, long the world's busiest airport, cannot keep growing to meet increased demand. The O'Hare facility occupies less than 3,200 hectares and its expansion is considered politically and environmentally difficult. Similarly, Chicago Midway cannot, according to TAMS, be expanded airside, nor can its existing single runway support long-haul operations.

To find the ideal location, TAMS reviewed six sites in north-east Illinois and northwest Indiana, and in December 1992 the Governor of the State of Illinois selected a rural site 60 kilometres south-west of the Chicago loop. It encompasses 9,650 hectares and is intended to take maximum advantage of existing roads while minimising impact on nearby settlements.

The new airport is built to meet forecasts that enplanements in the Chicago area will double in the next twenty years or so. According to TAMS, it is a 'supplemental' airport, comparable in function with Washington Dulles, London Gatwick and Paris Charles de Gaulle, though the rise of the last was based on closing the nearby Le Bourget and restricting use of Orly, south of Paris.

The ultimate SSA configuration is to include:

- four parallel runways spaced 1,524 metres apart to support four simultaneous instrument approaches;
- two dependent runways used only for departures in peak activity periods;
- a perimeter taxiway system which avoids run way incursions and minimises taxiing time. There is also a shorter crosswind runway to accommodate commuter aircraft.

Landside construction is planned around a central terminal with linear remote satellites, similar to the configuration at Atlanta–Hartsfield and Denver International. Serving the terminal building will be the usual split-level road approaches for arrivals and departures, with double entry and departure points for each level. The satellites will be served by dual people mover tunnels that allow longer satellites while keeping walking distances down. This configuration can be expanded in modules to accommodate well over the thirty million enplanements forecast for 2020.

In aerial views and layout plans, the number of runways and taxiways disguises the immense size of the main terminal and its satellites. Like Renzo Piano's Kansai International Airport in Osaka Bay, this new airport creates an impression through the use of long, low lines and a simple structural rhythm.

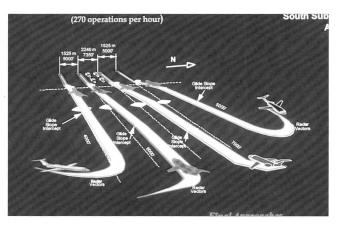

CINCINNATI AIRPORT, TERMINAL 3

Northern Kentucky, US

Cincinnati/Northern Kentucky Airport was already Delta Airlines' most profitable hub after Atlanta when the decision was taken to invest $180 million in new facilities. In view of the city's claim to lie within an hour's flying distance of sixty-two per cent of the American population, such expansion is inevitable. Here Delta has its own terminal, Terminal 3, linked by underground train and walkways to island Concourses A and B. The new facility opened in 1994.

The architects, THW, originally worked in accordance with the Atlanta plan, in which the terminal is sited at one end and linear transportation is run to successive island concourses. However, they concluded that such a layout hampered ease of orientation. If passengers missed the signs it would be just as easy to end up at a concourse further out when they merely wished to progress to baggage claim. This lack of orientation could have serious consequences for passengers with connecting flights.

The perennial problem, according to THW, is that once passengers enter many airports their exact location may not be clear: without constant reference to signs, there is no way of checking their bearings. At Cincinnati, the architects' guiding principle has been that passengers should be aware of their route. The link between parking decks, terminal and concourses runs through the middle of each building and is emphasised by glass skylights, clerestories and windows. This enables passengers to locate their destination and their aircraft as they move through the airport. As Witte explains, regardless of one's height the ceiling is always in view, and changes in materials, colour and form communicate the location.

The terminal is very open, with ticketing situated above and baggage claim below. Passengers who have tickets but no baggage can bypass the terminal completely, going direct from the parking zone through a security check to the transportation mall.

A tight budget meant that the new terminal had to be a basic structure, virtually a warehouse. THW has sought to give it individuality by adopting a Cincinnati theme, that of the great bridges across the Ohio River. 'We used industrial architecture. The roof deck and the mechanical systems are all exposed as in a warehouse', says Witte; structural elements are designed to suggest bridges. The terminal also incorporates five huge mosaic tile murals that were originally in the Cincinnati train terminal and later moved to the old air terminal building. The architects developed a hierarchy of wall finishes. Metal cladding or masonry was used where surfaces were vulnerable to damage or scuffing from baggage or maintenance carts, while the area above might simply be painted. Outside, aluminium panels were used in public areas; where there is less visibility, lower cost stainless steel panels were used.

Beneath each concourse is a cavernous concrete hall with a highly automated baggage system capable of handling 2,500 bags a minute. This is run from a control room at the top of the hall.

Equally impressive are the communication links. The subway train has been supplied by Otis Elevators and is a new application of its elevator technology. The new people movers glide on a thin cushion of air, pulled back and forth along the tunnel by a cable. At both ends are giant wheels and huge counterweights that drop 10 metres below this sub-grade level. The cars, which are linked in threes and can move 6,000 people an hour, are claimed to be more stable than trains that run on traditional tracks. The main propulsion motors are at both ends rather than on the trains themselves.

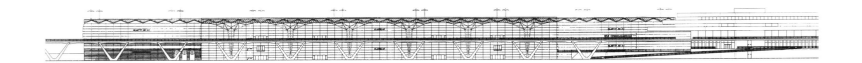

FROM ABOVE: South-west section; aerial view of model; north-west section; OPPOSITE: Model details and computer-generated perspectives

MURPHY/JAHN
COLOGNE/BONN AIRPORT, NORTH TERMINAL
Germany

This ambitious three-phase plan for a passenger terminal, roadway and parking garage, begins with the construction of a new north terminal (to open in 2000) attached to the existing one. The present terminal is in the form of a splayed U with a Parkhaus in the centre. The two piers linked to the corners of the U are six-point stars with an airbridge attached to each point. The existing terminal steps towards the centre and the height of the new building is restricted accordingly.

While the present terminal is largely a solid mass of terraces, the new structure is as transparent as possible, with floor-to-roof glazed sides, rising from ground level departures to the very inside of the eaves at departures level. Building components are exposed throughout: steel 'tree' columns with branches spreading from four-leg, structures, akin to those pioneered by Sir Norman Foster at London Stansted, reach up to support what is unmistakably the underside of the roof. This simple saw-tooth roof extends some way over the roadway to form a canopy.

The other appealing feature of the open design is the diagonal arrangement of the columns, which creates the effect of a wood planted quincunx fashion. Seen in section, the branches of the trees are significantly less vertical than those at Stansted, creating the impression of a cantilever bridge.

C W FENTRESS, J H BRADBURN AND ASSOCIATES

DENVER INTERNATIONAL AIRPORT, NEW TERMINAL

Colorado, US

The new $3.2 billion Denver Airport opened on 28 February 1995, following prolonged teething problems with its baggage handling system; problems which reverberated around the world to the delight of cynics and competitors. These problems have been solved, and although among the twenty busiest airports in the US, Denver now records the lowest level of delays and the new terminal can take its place alongside Kansai International and Chek Lap Kok as one of the world's finest new airports.

First, some statistics. Denver International is immense. It occupies a 13,700 hectare site, linked to the city by a new 37 kilometre highway. It has five 3,650-metre runways, with plans for a sixth, which will be 4,880 metres long. None of the runways intersects, minimising the chance of delay. The 100-metre control tower is the tallest in America.

The new Jeppersen terminal (named after the maker of Jepp navigational charts used by pilots) is connected by underground train to three island concourses with a total of ninety-four gates. Passengers can proceed to Concourse A on moving walkways along an enclosed bridge. This is set high enough to allow aircraft to taxi beneath and goes past the airport hotel and a ten-storey administration block. The baggage system, claimed to be the world's most complex,

comprises 32 kilometres of track and is equipped with 3,500 luggage carts.

Denver's former Stapleton Airport had been plagued by weather problems. At the new airport, a low-level windshear alert system, with twenty-nine wind speed and direction sensors on the airfield, has helped reduce the new airport's average delay rate.

The roof of the new terminal, inspired by the silhouette of the Rocky Mountains, is the largest tensile membrane roof in the world. It is formed by an arrangement of thirty-four 'peaks' organised in two rows, rising to some 40 metres in height. Its outer membrane is waterproof, using Teflon-coated fibreglass, while the inner membrane is of uncoated fibreglass. The white surface reflects ninety per cent of the high altitude sunlight and the fabric has so little mass that it does not conduct or store heat. Of the available light, ten per cent passes through.

The terminal is symmetrical on a central axis – one half of the building is the mirror of the other. There are six levels. Departures are on the upper level, Level 6. The vehicle drop-offs are not the usual viaducts but form the top level of the multi-level car parks that extend out from the terminal along both flanks, and descend a further two levels below ground. Additional tensile canopies shelter the roadway and passengers enter ticket

Conceptual sketch

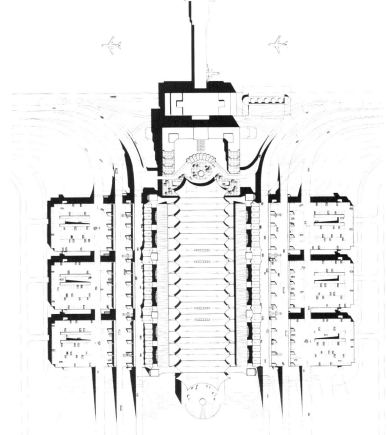

Site plan

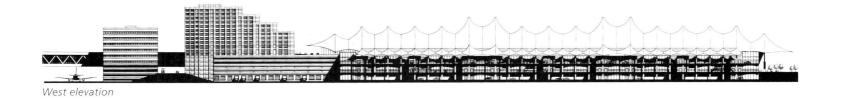

West elevation

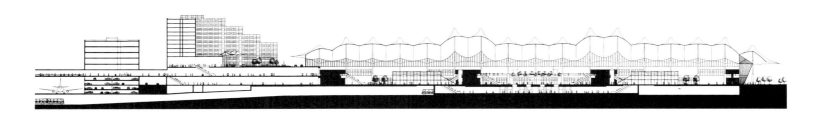

Longitudinal section

halls running the length of either side. The west ticketing hall is largely taken up by United Airlines, the airport's main user; the east hall by other airlines. The overwhelming majority of flights catered for are domestic.

Moving on, passengers arrive at balcony level overlooking the vast Great Hall which fills the centre of the terminal. From here they can progress straight to the departure concourses or they can descend to the floor of the Great Hall. Baggage claim is on the east and west sides of Level 5, exiting into roadways and pick-up points running the length of either flank. Level 5 roadways are reserved for taxis, limousines, shuttle buses and coaches. Passengers being picked up by private vehicles descend to a further set of road-ways and pick-up points on either side of Level 4.

Evidently, this is an airport designed for the convenience of car users, with over 13,200 carparking spaces provided in five-level garages on either side – though even these are proving insufficient. There is a whole hierarchy of parking. Long-term (economy) carparking spaces are provided east and west of the parking garages, served by a shuttle service that runs every ten minutes. Covered parking is provided at Levels 1 to 5 – east and west. Short-term, two-hour parking is provided on either side of Level 4 and is suitable for people collecting arriving passengers. There is no charge for a stay of up to seventy minutes. Curb-side check-in facilities for luggage and skis are provided on both Level 6, for people arriving by private car, and on Level 5, for passengers arriving by bus, taxi or shuttle. As an extra convenience, passengers can check in luggage at the curbside, go and park and return to Level 6 for ticketing.

Arriving at Denver has been compared to flying into a shopping mall. In 1997, the *San Francisco Chronicle* reported that the airport was earning so much rent from its restaurants, stores and parking spaces that it was cutting its landing fees by sixteen per cent.

In terms of architectural impact, the beauty and romance of Denver Airport lies in its tented fabric roofs. These are ranged in two perfectly matching rows, each line rising and falling in a symmetrical rhythm A-B-B-B-B-C-C-B-B-B-C-C-B-B-B-B-A. In

this rhythm, the As are at the end extending to form canopies; the Bs are the most numerous and the Cs form the high peaks, not only taller but marked out by skylights – in the forms of rings of windows suggestive of flying saucers. The idea was to evoke the peaks of the Rockies which rise like a wall at the back of the high tableland on which Denver sits, or, again, a cluster of Native American teepees. Precisely because these are tent roofs they are not 100 per cent even and the effect is highly picturesque. The stretched fabric between each pair of roofs forms a saddle, and creates a series of undulating forms akin to sand dunes or snow drifts.

Initially there was scepticism over the viability of the structure – cartoons depicted a 'Barnum & Bailey airport', and showed Denver's mayor struggling to hold down a section being blown off by a gust. The architects had considered sculpted concrete echoing Eero Saarinen's termi-nals at Dulles and JFK, but turned to tensile fabric partly to meet tight construction schedules. While some roofing systems required replacing every fifteen years, Teflon-coated fibreglass was consid-ered to have a life of upwards of thirty years. The oldest existing tensile structure using Teflon-coated fibreglass is at La Verne University in California: it dates from the early 1970s and remains in sound condition.

The roof was designed with the engineers Severud Associates of New York, with Horst Berger acting as principal designer and Edward M De Paola as project manager. Construction began with the erection of masts, held in position by erection cables. Crews first installed the top rings of the masts, then the mast-top units with solid enclosures for standard masts and glass enclo-sures for the high masts. This was followed by installation of the fabric/cable membrane system, starting from the north end. Sections were assem-bled on the ground, lifted into position and connected to masts and anchors. Stressing of the membrane followed.

'The feeling of being inside a giant pillowcase, which is typical of many fabric structures, was something we wanted to eliminate,' says Fentress. It was decided, therefore, to introduce large areas of glass wall, providing a constant

South elevation

Cross section

view of the sky. The glass wall rises to 18 metres and, as the fabric roof floats over it, appears to be freestanding, though in fact it receives some horizontal support from the roof system. To close the gap between the rigid walls and the flexible membrane roof, the architects and engineers designed a system of air-filled fabric. A pump system keeps the tubes inflated. When winds impose heavy loads, pressure can be released through valves. The roof is designed to sustain deformations of up to a metre in heavy wind or snow, but the deflection above the glazed wall is only 76 millimetres.

The canopies cantilevered over the drop-off points are almost 305 metres in length and are supported by piers set at 9-metre intervals, widening to 18 metres over the main entrances. Horizontal and vertical struts on top of the piers hold the membrane up and out; ties between the piers hold the structure down. These tie-down points also provide run-offs for rain and melting snow.

Due to Colorado's high altitude, ultraviolet radiation is high and low-emission glass is used to protect interior finishes against degradation and fading. At night the roofs glow invitingly. The hall is lit by up-lights contained in sconces wrapped round the pillars, with additional downlights clustered at the top of the columns.

The central feature of the terminal is the Great Hall, measuring 275 by 70 metres in length. The two rows of columns supporting the roof are 50 metres apart, the majority rising to 35 metres in height.

The three island concourses are situated to the north of the terminal – provision has been made for matching expansion to the south. Passengers can travel to the satellite by shuttle trains which depart from Level 4 every two minutes and descend under the apron, taking less than five minutes to reach Concourse C. Each concourse contains restaurants, shops and cash machines. International travellers arrive on Concourse A and clear customs on their way to the terminal.

One of the great triumphs of Denver is its successful programme of public art. The theme is the journey. On display are 'paper' planes, sky-bridge balustrades, pictograms set in the floor, musical chimes, bronze gargoyles and, most exciting, a kinetic light sculpture consisting of 5,280 metal propellers set in motion by the tunnel train to the concourse. The focal point of the atrium is a cactus and palm tree garden installed by Denver Botanic Garden.

This marvellous building requires just one brief warning: its perfect symmetry makes it important to know what side of the terminal you need, particularly when it comes to looking for your car!

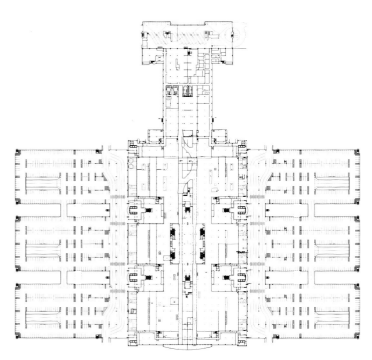

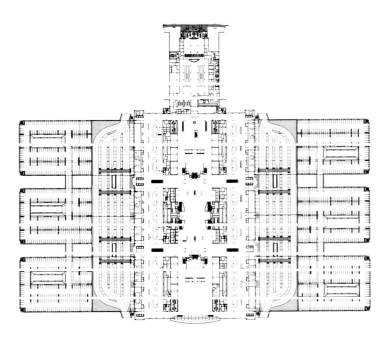

LEFT TO RIGHT: Fourth level plan; fifth level plan

FROM ABOVE: Exterior details; night-time elevation; aerial view; model

DOHA INTERNATIONAL AIRPORT, NEW TERMINAL
Qatar

The architects won the competition for a new twenty-gate passenger terminal at Doha International Airport in 1996 and the design was finalised in 1997. Qatar is a small but thriving Gulf state, with connections all over the Middle East. In form, the new terminal has echoes of Kansai, albeit on a reduced scale, with a central wave roof departure and arrival hall, and a long linear concourse with additional gates wrapped round the ends.

Visually, the terminal is not wholly characterised by athletic engineering and transparency since it evolves from a sustained response to local tradition, making strong use of colour and pattern. Certainly, a considerable amount of glass has been used, but there is also a feeling for mass, with positively Art Deco towers marking the gates and airbridges. These towers are based on traditional Qatari wind towers which helped to cool buildings during scorching summers by channelling a steady stream of air. The new airport towers contain mechanical air-cooling plant.

In the landside terminal, the arrivals area is situated at the lower level, with a broad ramped road leading up to departures. An imposing row of giant steel ribs, painted white, rises to support the oversailing roof. Their dramatic effect is enhanced as they rise from the pavement and not from the wall of the building. An exuberant delight in colour and pattern is at once evident in the paving, the glass and even the steel beams supporting the roof.

The check-in hall (measuring 110 by 52 metres) has an impressive vaulted roof: bold intersecting white beams are inset with glass panels admitting shafts of sunlight. The flattened arches of the roof are supported at just two points from square pillars sprouting round columns – a wayward touch but one in line with Fentress' penchant for inventing his own column forms, as at Denver. Beyond the departures hall is a retail mall punctuated by three circular towers (akin to the watch towers of arab forts such as Fort Zukar in Qatar). Here they provide the headroom for lofty palm trees and allow natural light into the mall.

The 348-metre-long airside concourse offers an impressive perspective of elliptical arches, its length to be emphasised by the regularly spaced palm trees. Again there is a strongly coloured, boldly patterned floor. Fentress explains:

> The design of the granite floors is inspired by traditional Qatari patterns reinterpreted in a modern way. Red for the sand, white for the local architecture and blue-grey for the waters of the Gulf. The stones used in the arrival and departure hall are opposites – so where white is used in the arrival hall, red is found in the corresponding position in departures. This allows us to use intricate shapes without wasting stone.

Harmonising with Fentress' colour rationale, the exterior is faced with large, metre-square porcelain tiles with a white plaster finish to the concrete surface above.

The half-level placement of the airbridges enables passengers to walk down rampways from departures and also down to arrivals. Estimated to cost $100 million, the projected opening date of the airport is set for August 2000.

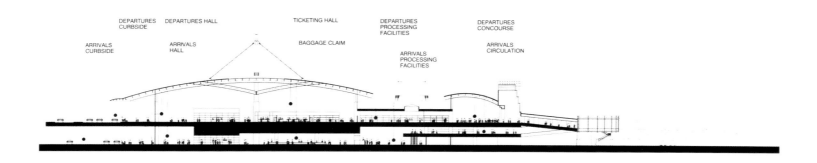

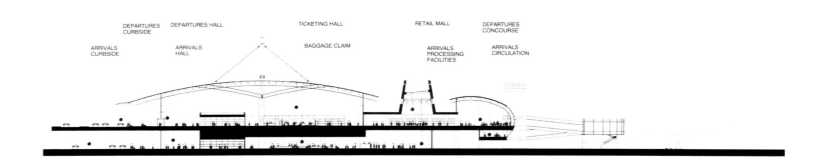

FROM ABOVE: Curb-side perspective; sections

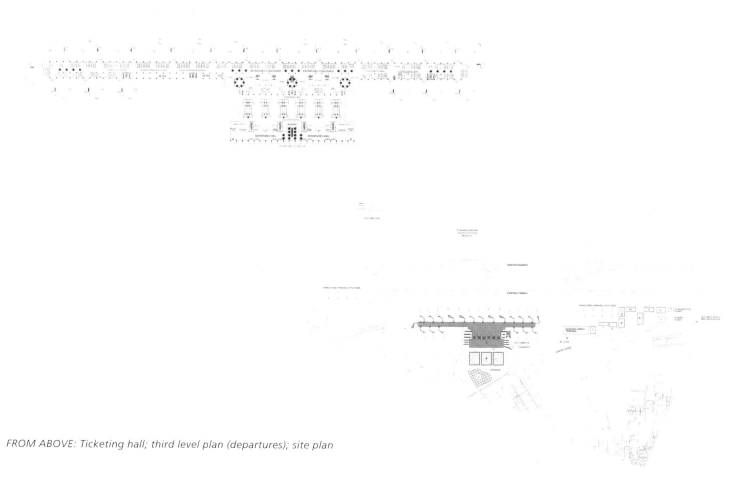

FROM ABOVE: Ticketing hall; third level plan (departures); site plan

FRANKFURT AIRPORT, TERMINAL 2
Germany

Opened on 24 October 1994, Frankfurt Airport ranks as Europe's second largest international hub after London Heathrow. Situated at the heart of western Europe, it now serves an increasing number of East European destinations.

Since nearly half of all passengers transfer to other flights, Frankfurt seeks to guarantee transfer times of only forty-five minutes, including transfers between terminals. As the new Terminal 2 is some distance from the existing Terminal 1, fast transfer of both passengers and baggage was critical. This has been achieved as a result of the airport's highly efficient baggage conveyor system and a new elevated people mover system called Skyline.

The terminal is an impressive 600 metres long, 100 metres wide and more than 30 metres high. It has been designed to handle a peak capacity of more than ten million passengers a year so it has correspondingly spacious gate lounges. Subterranean floors include an underground car park for 4,500 vehicles.

From the check-in hall (Level 2), escalators lead to the departure level (Level 3). Level 2 also houses the arrival area with passport control, baggage reclaim and customs. Level 1, situated below the check-in hall, houses baggage handling, workshops and airline facilities, as well as bus gates. Level 4 accommodates cafeterias, snack bars, restaurants, a visitor terrace and the PTS shuttle station for the rail link between the two terminals.

The architects conceived the new terminal as a place of encounter, a large busy concourse. The overall impression they have sought to create is one of lavish space, with clear and simple orientation for passengers. Transparency, light and air are the keynotes. Both inside and out the terminal has a smart livery of greys – pearl grey, dove grey and elephant grey – shades very much akin to Foster & Partners' favoured palette. Nonetheless,

the treatment of glass and steel is altogether different from Foster's work. The aim here is not so much to achieve an elegant minimalism but rather positive robustness. All the structural elements contribute to this effect, from roof trusses to window framing.

The great arched trusses of the roof also provide a clear visual association with the imposing iron and glass roofs of Frankfurt's vast and imposing Hauptbahnhof, one of the great railway termini of Europe. The lofty roofs and walls of glass provide panoramic views over the airport from upper levels, of aircraft taking off, landing and taxiing to and from gates.

Seen from an arriving plane taxiing towards an airbridge, the airport has a glacial quality – smooth, reflective and cool in colour, yet for all the great expanse of glass it is far from transparent. Virtually every surface in view is glass; more memorable because the building is not one sheer curtain-wall of glass from tarmac to roof, but stepped out in great blocks back and forth.

The other eye-catching feature of the new terminal is the use of advertisements to bring colour and animation to the large concourses. These are often abhorred by architects because they interrupt or clash with the clean lines of an interior. Here, by suspending them from the roof like great banners, Perkins & Will makes them a positive feature. On the main concourses are large 'action areas' for staging events and exhibitions. Shopping is intended to appeal to both air passengers and local people.

The provision of only eight aircraft docking positions in front of the building has been criticised. However, the terminal is intended primarily for wide-bodied aircraft serving the North Atlantic and Asian routes and a further eighteen apron positions can be accessed from the building.

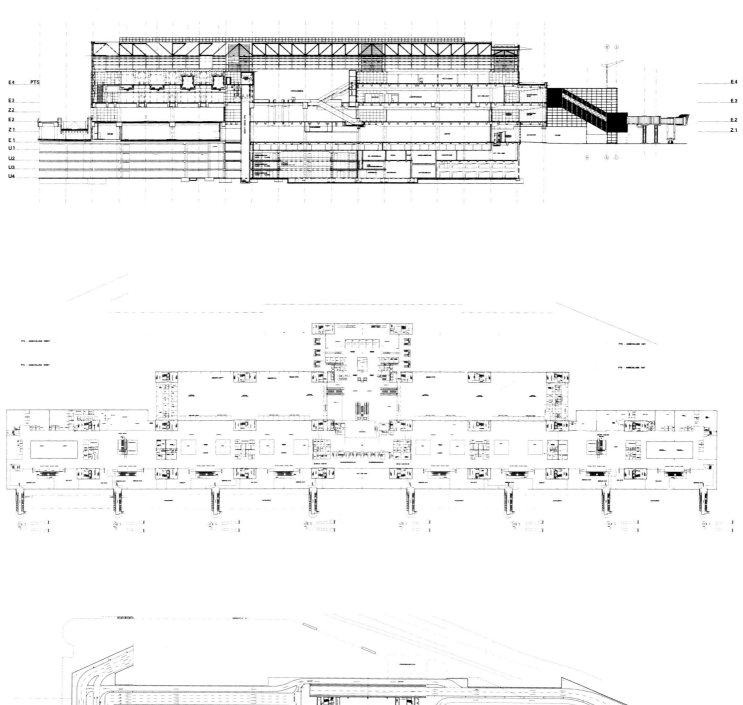

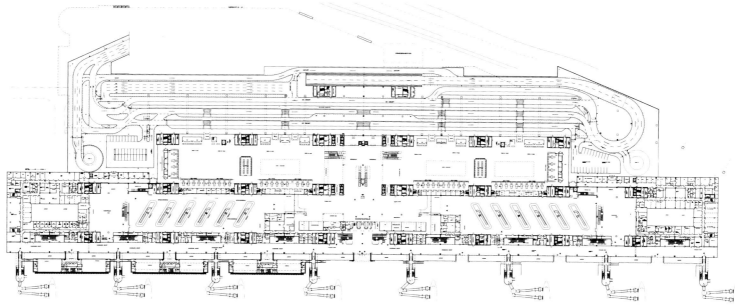

FROM ABOVE: Cross section; fourth level plan; second level plan

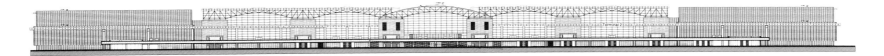

North elevation

South elevation

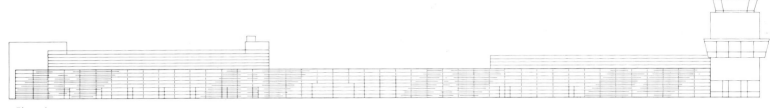

Elevation

FLORIAN RIEGLER AND ROGER RIEWE
GRAZ INTERNATIONAL AIRPORT, NEW TERMINAL
Austria

The competition in 1989 to design an extension to Graz's airport was won by Riegler and Riewe, with construction commencing in October 1992. Completion and inauguration occurred in October 1994. The elegant new terminal is a superb example of the long low lines that graced the pioneering works of Modernism.

The brief was to extend and upgrade the existing airport building, originally constructed to handle a capacity of 350,000 passengers a year, which forecasts indicated would double to 700,000. According to the architects, such an increase in passenger numbers prompted a single level solution as 'two-level solutions are generally not economically viable with less than one million passengers a year'. From the existing airport buildings, only the tower, some of the offices and the restaurant were preserved. The first phase comprised building the new check-in and departure areas without touching the old ones. In the second phase the old airport was demolished and replaced by new arrivals and baggage claim areas.

The alterations involved increasing the depth of the building and lowering the roof, barely changing the length so as to allow for future expansion. The architects conceived the airport as a place of transfer and adopted the guiding principle of making this aspect as simple as possible.

Visibility and transparency are the initial means. The continuous glazing on the landside is set well back beneath a 7-metre roof cantilever. This is intended to reduce reflections, allowing a clear view of the interior. Large sheets of floor-to-ceiling glass set in the slenderest stainless steel framing increase the sense of openness. The entrance doors are immediately obvious as they project forward and are edged in metal. The canopy projects well over the drop-off lane so that anyone alighting from either side of a car in the rain will be under cover. Plentiful light is provided by numerous roof fittings into which electric lights are neatly housed.

Riegler and Riewe do not believe in structural expressionism and the suspended ceiling inside the airport is continued outside. Theirs is not an architecture which seeks to create metaphors of flight, nevertheless in the gentle upward slope of the canopy and the rounded forward edge there is just a hint of an aircraft wing.

Part of the beauty of this building is that the division between outside and inside is blurred. The chequer pattern of skylights continues in the check-in hall and the white terrazzo floor was chosen to reflect light back to the ceiling. The largest possible slabs have been laid, measuring 5 by 3 metres. The roof structure was developed to create the maximum spans, thereby allowing flexibility in the future.

Landside and airside are strongly contrasting. Arriving passengers see a 160-metre-long facade emblazoned with four giant letters announcing GRAZ. At closer view it is evident these have been cut out from a series of aluminium bands so they read equally well at night when illuminated from behind. Here, three sheets of glass provide additional acoustic protection.

Light and transparency are also the hallmarks of the offices situated at one end of the new building. The central corridor, attractively planted with bamboo, is surrounded by glass in every direction – glass walls to the offices, glass bridges linking the upper floor and a glass roof.

Riegler and Riewe's work is characterised by simple rectangular forms, in plan, section and elevation, where the set square, not the compass, always reigns. Its appeal evolves from their unerring sense for line and proportion.

Elevation

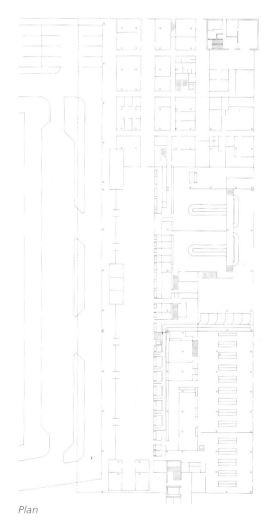

Plan

VON GERKAN • MARG & PARTNER

HAMBURG AIRPORT, TERMINAL 4

Germany

Hamburg's monumental new terminal adds a positively theatrical element to departures, not just through the sheer scale and boldness of design, but by creating a sense of 'onwards and upwards' as the traveller proceeds from check-in to the departure gate. It is very much a development of Meinhard von Gerkan's 'supershed' at Stuttgart (completed in 1991), where the roof is also angled upwards towards the airside.

At Hamburg, the terminals have developed in linear fashion along the apron. Terminals 1A and 1B are now used for charter flights. The crescent-shaped red brick Terminal 2 (now disused) was added to the south, then Terminal 3, and now von Gerkan's new Terminal 4. The masterplan provides for the new concourse to be doubled in size and then almost doubled again. For this reason, the pier leading to the departure gates extends in one direction only – serving the earlier terminals and allowing the extensions to replace them on the same side, so walking distances will be reduced considerably. At the end, the pier swings out in a curve, not just out of bravura, but allowing the charter hall to be retained.

On the landside, the roof descends low over the drop-off point, projecting beyond the pavement over the road, so that access to or from cars, or unloading luggage, is protected from driving rain. Inside, the vast roof, spanning an area 75 by 101 metres, is supported by just twelve stout concrete columns. It is the more dramatic for being raised aloft, first on tubular beams (tapering to pointed ends like giant knitting needles) and then on giant arch trusses which span the space from side to side.

The outer walls (landside and airside) are of clear glass, as if to emphasise the lack of other structural supports. These supports are symmetrically placed, but on the airside the columns rise not from ground level but from two levels higher so that internally the roof appears to be ascending almost the whole time it is in view.

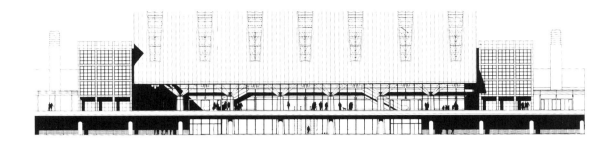

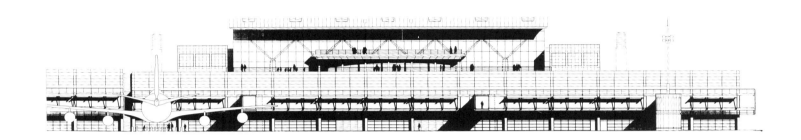

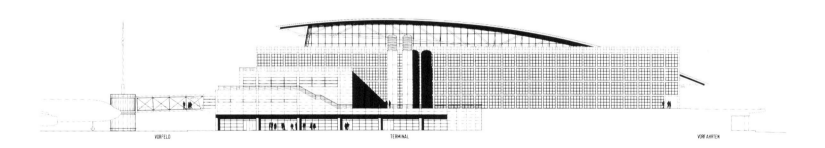

VORFELD   TERMINAL   VORF AHRTEN

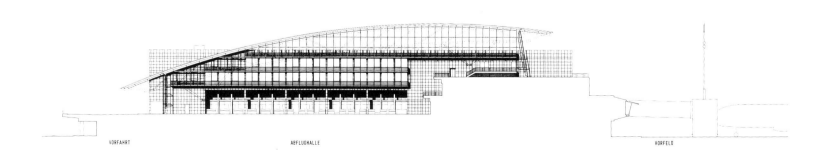

VORFAHRT   ABFLUGHALLE   VORFELD

Elevations

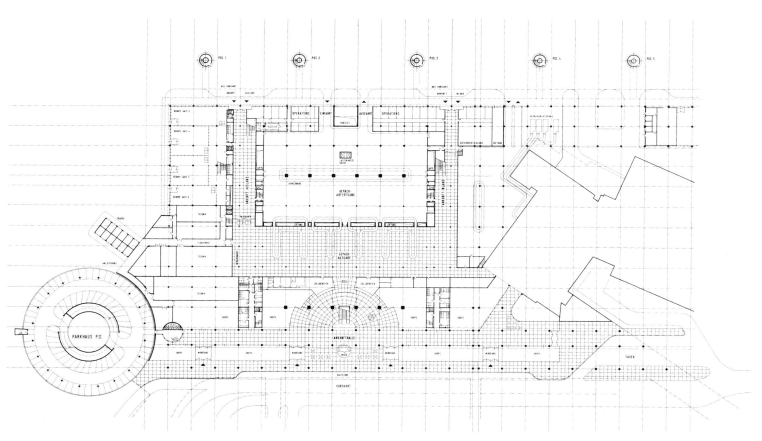

Plan

The most significant feature of much German Baroque architecture is the staircase hall, or *Treppenhaus*, a huge ceremonial space filling the centre of a building, with twin flights ascending ceremonially and symmetrically to a *piano nobile*, overlooked by balconies or galleries where people can gather. This arrangement occurs at Hamburg, where the architects have ensured that passengers progress visibly through the space and form an enlivening throng, animating the departures hall at different levels.

The ground level arrivals hall has, of necessity, lower ceilings and artificial lighting but in the centre it opens up into the departure hall above, surrounded by a large semi-circular balcony. Twin escalators, flanked by steps, make an axial ascent. There is also a lift in a glass drum for the convenience of passengers with trolleys. Check-in facilities are provided on symmetrically placed twin islands, which are low and without vertical partitions, preserving the all-important sense of openness.

Shops, restaurants and bars are distributed on three levels at the airside end, accessed by escalators. The first upper level has a cafe, complete with umbrellas, intended to create an al fresco feel – they may be of perforated metal but this does not look out of place. For the traveller, or the day visitor, the appeal lies in having a choice of distinctly different places to eat and drink – Europa Buffet, Red Wings, Top Air.

Arriving passengers, after passing through immigration, proceed to the baggage hall with its unusual ceiling that is reminiscent of the fireproof vault of a nineteenth-century mill, with parallel shallow arch vaults. Throughout, a smart grey colour scheme dominates, with both stone and metal walling – the architects have a distinct penchant for perforated metals, grilles and gauze.

The main upper-level cafe leads out on to a spacious open air terrace overlooking the apron and is immensely popular in good weather. Above the cafe is an extra mezzanine level that can be opened up at busy times. Public telephones are a

model of their kind, each contained within a generous half globe of Perspex, which provides a sense of privacy and a degree of separation from the noise of the concourse.

On a dull day, the dominant battleship-grey steel-work of the departure hall is quite overpowering, though relief is provided by the beige panels of the roof. The weakest point of the design is the external roof cladding as seen on the landside. Its pale beige colour appears as if the wrong side up, and is not a fitting prelude to the powerful architecture within.

The airside, greeting the passenger arriving by plane, is much more distinctive. The eye is immediately attracted to the bright red steel-work of the airbridges, which span a wide apron service road. Simple X-braces emphasise the clean transparent lines. At the outer end these are supported by steel structures like the towers of a suspension bridge which transform the airbridges into a sculptural feature. The emphatic, overhanging sunshades protecting the floor-to-ceiling glass along the concourse add an exotic, almost oriental touch.

At baggage claim, as well as the customary trolleys, a sign announces that a porter service is available via the information desk. This can also be booked in advance by telephone or fax.

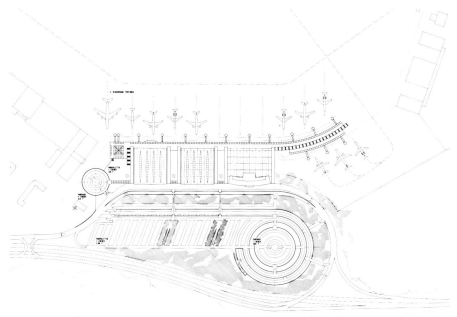

Plan

PEKKA SALMINEN ARCHITECT & ASSOCIATES LTD

HELSINKI–VANTAA AIRPORT, MIDDLE TERMINAL

Finland

This new terminal is being constructed in two phases: the first was from 1994–96, followed by the second phase, which is scheduled for completion in 1999. The terminal is situated on a triangular, wedge-shaped site formed by the intersection of two runways. The pointed corner provides the dynamic geometry for the whole complex, and the triangular motif is repeated in the layout of the interiors and the control tower. It also appears in details, most obviously in the triangular granite floor tiles and the large skylight prisms. These structures beam both natural and artificial light (by day and night) into the interior of the building.

The first phase, which opened in November 1996, forms a connection between the existing international and domestic terminals. Eight new or renovated departure gates are provided with passenger boarding bridges and two bus gates, all with their own departure lounges.

Passengers will be filtered principally through a shopping arcade with tax-free and speciality shops connecting to a triangular hall, providing information, catering and airline lounges. This hall offers that most welcome feature for transfer passengers faced with long waits or delays – a view of the apron and runway (through a two-storey high glass wall), offering the reassuring sight of planes arriving and taking off. The best look-out spot, at the corner, houses an à-la-carte restaurant with views of both runways.

The control tower, looming over the corner, has two levels – a circular 'air traffic' control room at the top, with 360-degree visibility, and immediately below, a beak-like projecting 'apron control' room with views over the apron on either side.

The new departure lounges at the top resemble conservatories: glass roofs and walls dispel the feeling that passengers are being corralled and give them a liberating dose of light and sunshine; or, when it rains, the sense of being safely indoors. Likewise, the glass sides of the airbridges avoid the claustrophobic feeling of approaching the plane through a tunnel. Transparent walls also offer arriving passengers a more inviting view of the terminal.

The second phase will increase the capacity of the terminal to six million passengers. The main feature will be a new triangular departure hall with a gently rising roof, supported by three columns branching out to carry space trusses. There is an intentional metaphor of take-off in the rise of the roof and the view of the skies provided through the widening windows.

The one potential criticism is the incessant use of grey through the interior (as if it wasn't ubiquitous in the 1980s and early 1990s). Subtle shades of elephant and dove grey may have been used to complement the stainless steel and polished granite surfaces but ultimately the use of so much grey can become monotonous.

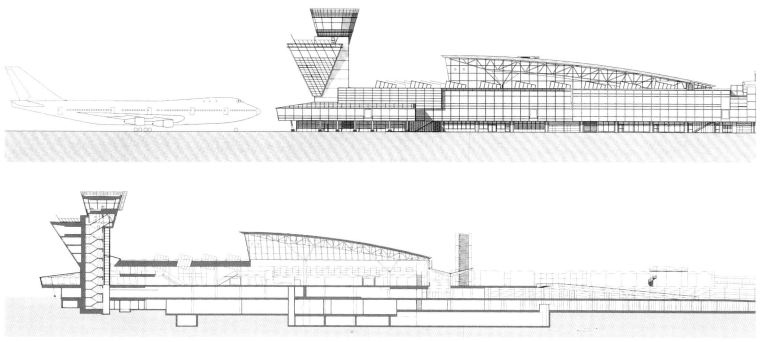

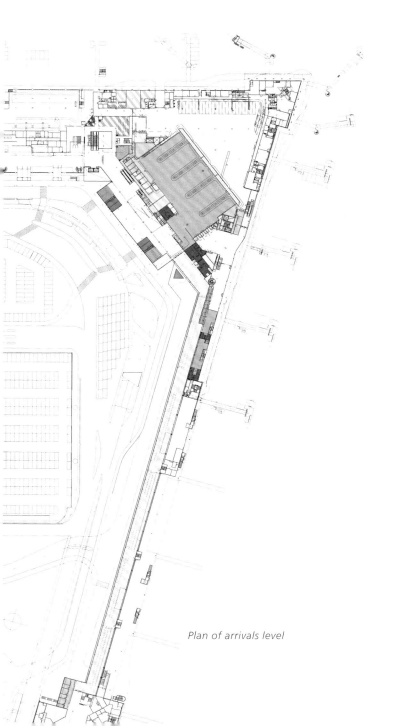

FROM ABOVE: North-west elevation; section

Plan of arrivals level

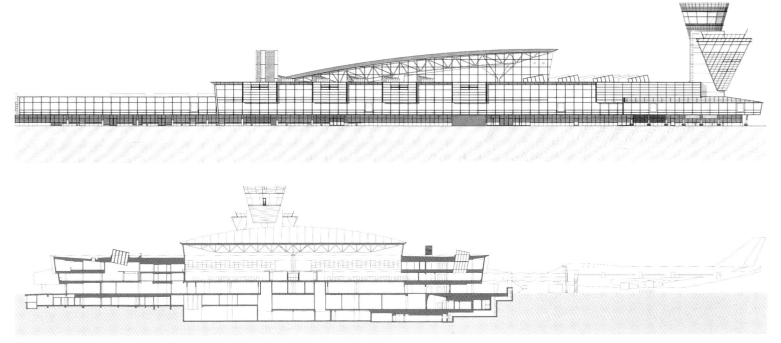

FROM ABOVE: North-east elevation; section

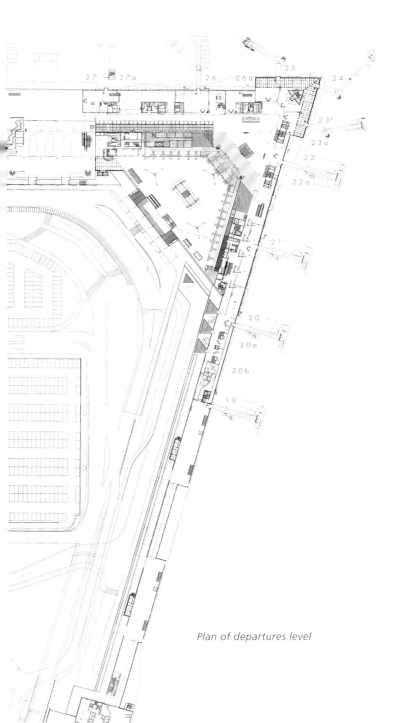

Plan of departures level

Model

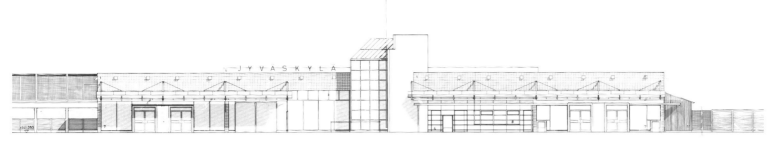

Elevation

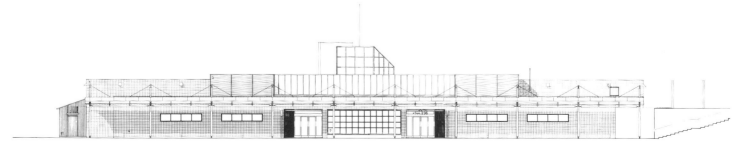

Elevation

JYVÄSKYLÄ AIRPORT, NEW TERMINAL

Finland

Finnish architecture is renowned the world over for elegance and lightness of touch. This is immediately evident at Jyväskylä Airport, one of the hubs of Finland's air traffic network. The terminal, which opened in 1988, handles some 300,000 domestic and international passengers with the result that recently, there has been an attempt to lighten the load at Helsinki–Vantaa Airport by increasing the number of international flights – particularly charter flights – at other airports.

Jyväskylä Airport was designed for scheduled flights and the new terminal is an addition to an existing building. The early 1960s terminal has been preserved and has been renovated to accommodate charter flights and office space. The new terminal is a simple one-storey pavilion.

The interior is divided into two sections, allowing simultaneous handling of two departures and two arrivals. To handle large charter flights sliding walls can be opened to create larger areas. The architects considered it especially important to create a feeling of spaciousness since this is a relatively small building serving large numbers of people. To this end, they have incorporated a large skylight and integrated a cafeteria with a glass tower, both intended to counter the impression of enclosed space by allowing the maximum amount of natural light to enter.

In response to the low budget, most of the structural elements and materials are standard components. The vertical structure is formed of in-situ concrete pillars and walls, the roof of beams and hollow-core slabs. The granite-grey, glazed ceramic tiles were evolved specially for the project. The steel canopies are intended to lighten the mass of the masonry, their wing-shape providing a subtle hint of *architecture parlante* – architecture that proclaims its purpose.

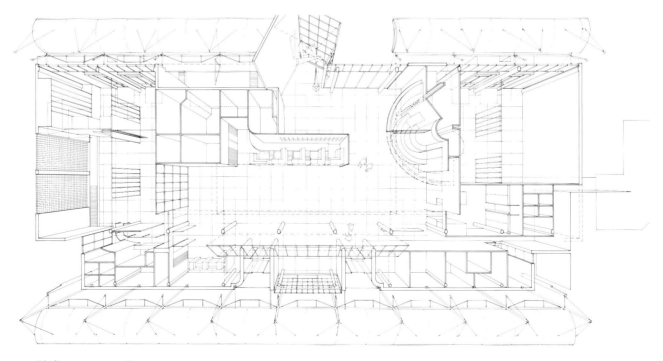

Bird's-eye perspective

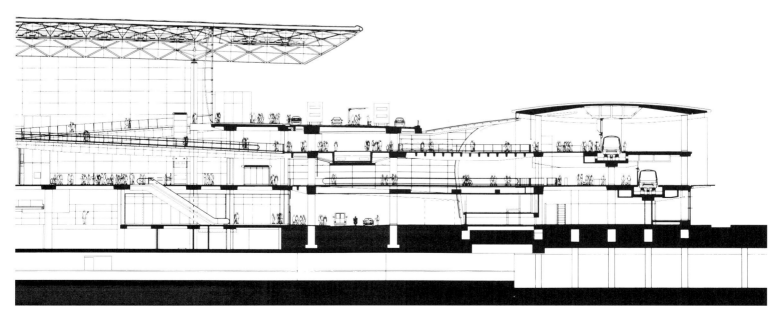

FROM ABOVE: Model view, section detail

CHEK LAP KOK AIRPORT

Lantau Island, Hong Kong

Half the world's population is within five hours' flying distance of Hong Kong and this wholly new airport was designed to provide for a massive increase in air traffic, fuelled by Asia's economic miracle. Hong Kong's Kai Tak Airport, famed for its hair-raising approach between the city's tower blocks, could not meet the needs of such a dramatic expansion, though its fast connections to downtown Hong Kong and Kowloon were valued by many. By contrast, Chek Lap Kok, planned to handle thirty-five million passengers a year in 1998, can expand to eighty-seven million on full completion in 2040.

The new airport is Hong Kong's answer to Singapore's facility, which is an imposing, spacious, efficient and calm airport that has greatly boosted Singapore's position as one of South-East Asia's principal hubs. The Pacific region is among the busiest in the world, and Hong Kong is among its top four centres, competing directly with Tokyo, Seoul and Singapore.

Built on reclaimed land along the northern coast of Lantau Island, the 1,248 hectare site of the new airport is 25 kilometres from the heart of Hong Kong. It is the size of the Kowloon Peninsula and four times larger than the old Kai Tak Airport, which is now to be reused for construction land. Formation of the platform began in December 1992, and by April 1994 sufficient land had been prepared to enable the first foundations to be laid for the passenger terminal, which was opened on 6 July 1998.

The terminal, with its Y-shaped concourse, is 1.27 kilometres long (in comparison with Kansai International Airport's 1.7 kilometres) and is located between the two runways at the north-eastern end of the island. The masterplan provides for an additional X-plan island concourse and a possible second terminal immediately on the

other side of the station for the express train coming into the airport.

Since it opened, the airport has had one runway operating round the clock without flight restrictions; a second was due to be completed in late 1998. The new terminal has thirty-eight airbridges as well as nineteen remote stands.

Fast, efficient transport is integral to the design and at Chek Lap Kok the terminal is claimed to be the first in the world to accommodate express rail-link trains inside the complex at both departure and arrival levels (incoming trains switch level on a spur beyond the platforms). Check-in facilities will also be provided at the new Kowloon Station, enabling passengers to shed their luggage even before they board the train. The journey will take twenty-three minutes, with trains running at eight-minute intervals. Passengers with luggage can also choose the coach that will allow them to alight closest to the airline check-in desk they seek.

Providing the communications to the new island airport has involved 34 kilometres of expressway, a mass transit rail link, a third cross-harbour tunnel and two major bridges, engineered by Mott Connell: one a cable stay bridge and the other the world's longest road–rail suspension bridge. The twin railtracks are contained in a steel box beneath the road. As the bridge can move up to a metre in strong winds, special expansion joints have been designed to cope with movement in the steel railway lines; when winds rise to Typhoon Force 8, and cars are banned from the bridge, trains can run undisturbed below.

Road approaches split into an elevated, upper departures level, and a lower ground-level artery serving arrivals. Car parks, which at many airports are so large that they prevent terminals being seen to advantage, are not intrusive. At Kai Tak there was little demand for long-term airport car

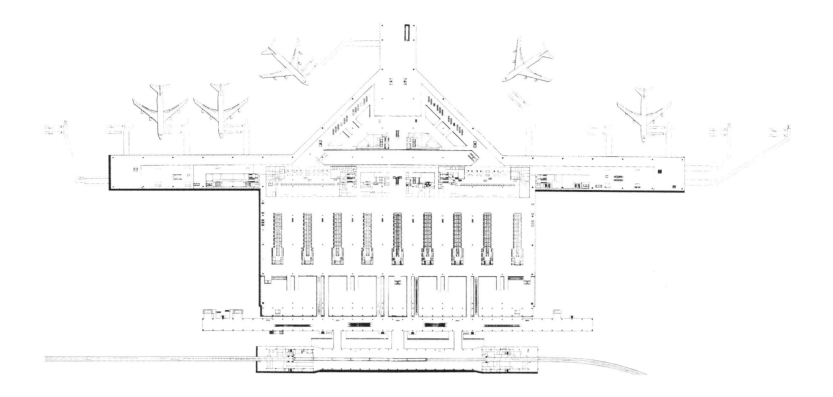

Plan of departures level

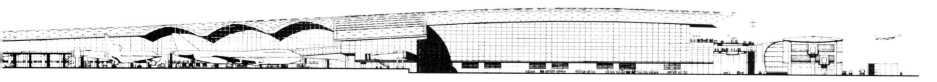

South elevation

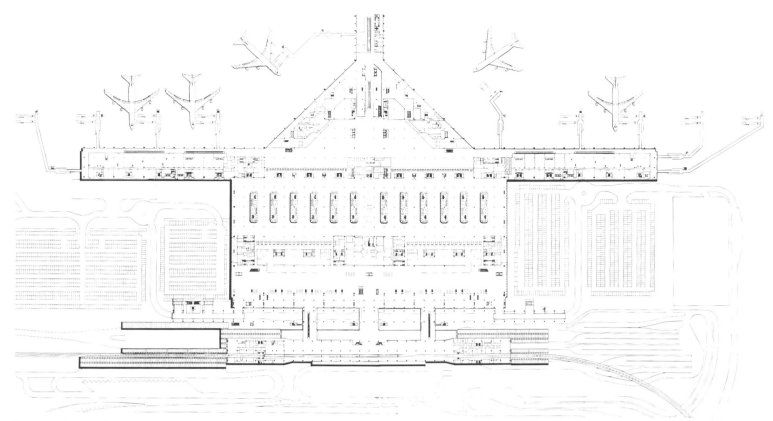

Plan of arrivals level

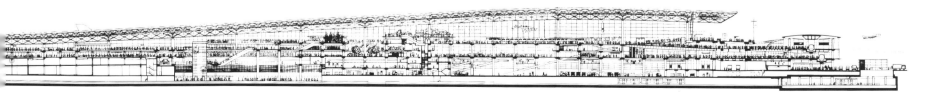

Longitudinal section

parking and only a modest amount has been provided here.

The architects' overriding aims have been simplicity and clarity. Foster explains:

> When people think of a major airport they think of several separate terminals. Here it is all in one building. If Canary Wharf was formed of building blocks you could drop the whole lot inside.

The terminal is the world's largest. It is air travel's version of New York's Grand Central Station, a building loftier and more cavernous than its predecessors. In the main departures level, which is covered by 18 hectares of roof, there is not one single cross wall or full-height partition. Like a great cathedral, it is one single continuous space rising to the roof vaults.

The spectacular sense of openness is increased by the continuous curtain-wall of glass. Its 5.5 kilometre length encircles the departures level and the arrivals hall, providing breathtaking panoramas of mountains, sky, sea, ships and islands, as well as the constant activity on the runway. Altogether, the wall incorporates 10,000 specially toughened sheets of glass, 3 metres wide and 2 metres high, ensuring that the first transom is fixed above everyone's line of vision.

At Stansted the roof is of uniform height throughout the terminal. Here it descends markedly towards the periphery, swooping down still further over the long concourse leading to the distant gates and so creating an effect like the snaking body of a Chinese carnival dragon.

While Stansted has 'trees' to support the roof, at Chek Lap Kok Foster has refined the structure down to columns of pencil-like proportions, set at impressive 36-metre intervals, which rise up to carry bowstring steel trusses spanning from column to column. The lattice ribs of the vault are inset with perforated acoustic panels.

At the upper departures level, all the roof vaults are inclined in one direction, creating visual clarity. 'The grain and angle of the structure provide instant orientation both inside and outside the building,' explains Foster. The overriding idea is that the planes and runway should be on view throughout the departures level, leaving no doubt as to which way to progress.

The 32,000 roof components were shipped to Hong Kong in 6 metre and 12 metre containers for assembly on site. The sections of arched vault, weighing up to 138 tonnes, were assembled on the tarmac, then balanced hydraulically as they were moved at walking pace to the building, lifted up by giant 500-tonne crawler cranes, then slid along the tops of the columns to the more central parts which the crane could not reach. The design was worked out with engineers Ove Arup.

Foster's brilliance lies in creating a building that is almost a kit of giant parts, enabling the terminal to be completed on time and well within budget. He remarks, 'It had to be made of relatively simple elements that could be simultaneously produced in Bolton or Singapore.' The seeming simplicity is enhanced by Foster's choice of colour palette: the interior is predominantly white and grey – white for the structural elements such as columns, with grey-honed granite for the concourse floors and the departure lounge carpets.

The whole design is intended to eliminate the frustrating changes of level that confront passengers at many airports. Entrance to the terminal, for both road and rail passengers, will be along a series of high-level ramped bridges set across the arrivals hall below. Foster's innovative concept means that check-in desks are not arranged in a long row across the back of the hall but in nine parallel ranges, allowing ticketed passengers to walk straight through to security and passport control. The architects hold that the 20 metres' distance between facing counters is sufficiently generous to avoid queues blocking the route.

After passing through passport control, passengers arrive in the East Hall, where a large balcony looks down to arrivals. They can then use the moving walkways to progress to the departure gates, or descend below apron level and take the passenger shuttle train which speeds them to the West Hall at the far end of the terminal in sixty seconds. (A proportion of passengers, including those flying with Cathay Pacific, Hong Kong's home airline, will go to 'near' gates immediately to the left and right of passport control.)

Arriving passengers, depending on the position of the airbridge, use the shuttle or moving walkways. Those landing at remote stands will be ferried by bus directly to the main

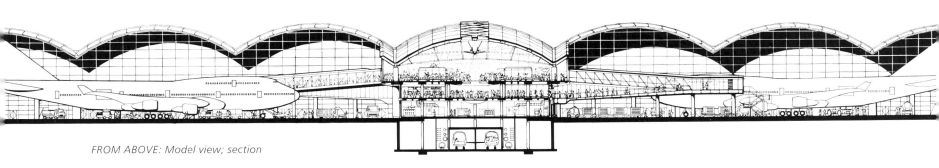

FROM ABOVE: Model view; section

Aerial view

terminal hall. Once they have passed immigration, they enter an impressive, columned double-height baggage collection hall, as wide as the departure hall above. Here, aligned naturally with passenger flow, is an array of twelve baggage carousels. Beyond is a large meeters-and-greeters hall.

In an age accustomed to fire doors blocking the way along every corridor and concourse, Foster has created what is in effect the world's largest officially approved and tested fire compartment. He explains:

As at Stansted, we have taken all the plant and ductwork which used to go on the roof of an air terminal and put it below. By doing this you create a structure where there is nothing left to burn.

Fire regulations have been met by extensive use of non-combustible materials – the concessions have not needed to be placed on a separate level to achieve this, as at Kansai, though shops and restaurants are equipped with roller shutters and water sprinklers. According to Graham Plant, head of engineering for the Hong Kong Airports, if a localised fire breaks out, the air conditioning stops and powerful smoke extractors suck smoke and fumes straight out through the roof.

A crucial factor, in terms of quality, is that Foster & Partners has been given full control over the interior, designing all the furniture, check-in islands and desks, for example. The entire layout of the terminal is a brilliant metaphor for flight – not overt but suggestive of a glider with a long thin fuselage and a swept-back tail.

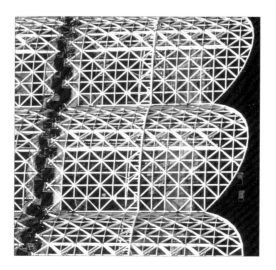

Roof geometry

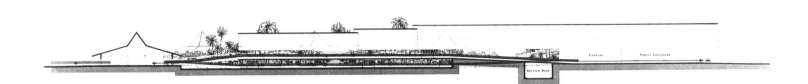

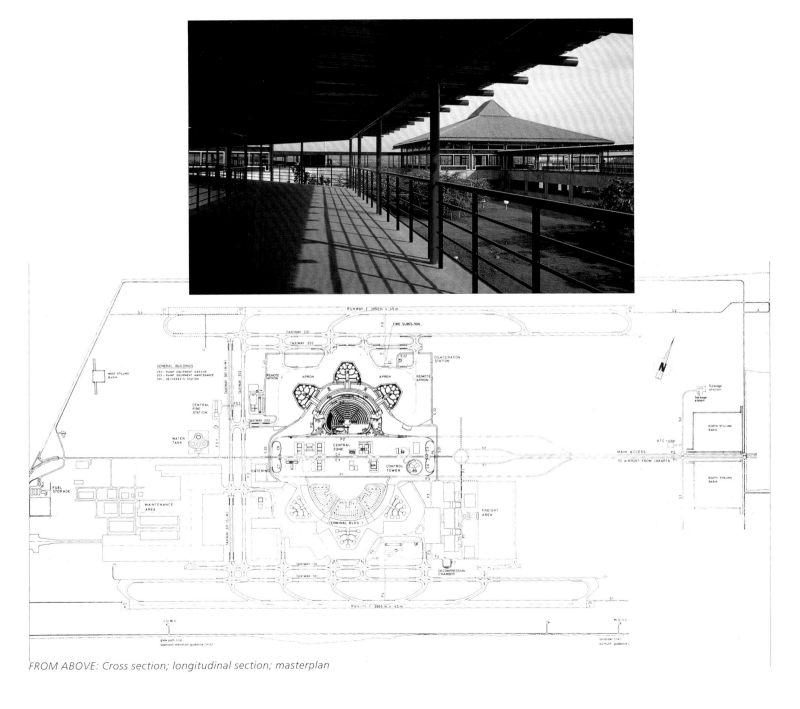

FROM ABOVE: Cross section; longitudinal section; masterplan

JAKARTA INTERNATIONAL AIRPORT
Indonesia

Jakarta International Airport, Soekarno-Hatta, began as the welcome exception to the modern trend towards enclosed, almost hermetically sealed, air-conditioned terminals. The architects recognised that fresh air as well as abundant daylight can be the key to creating pleasant spaces, so departure gates are approached along covered terrace walks, looking down on either side to gardens laid out with lawns, shrubs and bamboo.

The layout of this airport is another example of the mastery of grand symmetrical designs of Paul Andreu and his team. The main access road from Jakarta enters on the central long axis, and then branches to form a loop (similar to Terminals 2A–D at Charles de Gaulle, Paris) serving two facing terminals laid out in perfect symmetry on either side of the main axis.

Terminal Building 1 (Phase I) with three halls (two domestic and one international) was opened in 1984. Phase II was opened in 1990, with one domestic hall and one international hall. The plan echoes that of a seventeenth-century Vauban fortress with bastions on every side. The symmetry extends to the runways and taxiways which are almost mirror images of each other. Runway 1, at 3,665 metres, is longer than Runway 2 (3,050 metres). In the same way as hotel rooms are numbered by floor, the taxiways are numbered in sequence: 101 and 102 for Runway 1, for example, 201 and 202 for Runway 2 and 301 and 302 for the cross taxiways linking the two runways.

The departure gate lounges in the first phase take the form of square pavilions with shady roofs resting on columns. Passengers can sit in the cool of the pavilions or linger outdoors in the shade. Here they are above ground, at the level of the boarding gates, where they can take full advantage of any breeze. These pavilions have distinctive peaked roofs resting on rafters that recall the traditional bamboo roofs of Indonesian houses. The second phase echoes the design of the first, but somewhat sadly the airport authorities decided that passengers must remain indoors.

The approach roads curve round sharply in front of the crescent-shaped terminals, the spaces created inside the curves (almost a half circle) being laid out as surface car parks. From the departure halls, passengers proceed across bridges to the two bastion-like piers on which the pavilion lounges are set. Being five-sided they can accommodate the largest planes while keeping walking to a minimum. Up to eight planes can be parked around each pier. With the same rigorous French logic, stands are numbered sequentially according to pier, with the remote stands also arranged in sequence.

As far as possible, symmetry is maintained in the layout of airport roads – for example, in the filter roads off the main loop, while the main axial entrance road continues as a service road bisecting the whole layout. The exact symmetry is only broken by ancillary buildings, such as the freight and maintenance area, catering building and fuel farm but these, too, are laid out and designed in a strictly rectilinear fashion. Individual buildings are given distinct geometrical configurations, such as the propeller-shaped base of the control tower and the clover leaf arrangement of the water tanks.

Traffic rose from nine million passengers in 1985 to fourteen million five years later. In 1990, the completed terminals were provided with 134 check-in counters, twelve conveyor belts and fourteen electro-mechanical airbridges, six flap-system display boards and sixty-nine TV monitors. The project's estimated construction cost at 1980 prices was $120 million.

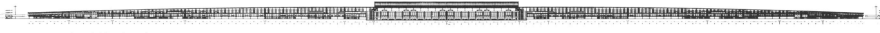

Landside elevation

KANSAI INTERNATIONAL AIRPORT

Osaka Bay, Japan

Aviation has given birth to no more spectacular building than the Kansai terminal. Intriguingly, its remarkable design is born, above all, of one idea, which came from that most experienced of all airport architects, Paul Andreu.

His vision was not to split domestic and international flights into separate terminals, or even opposite ends of the same one. Instead, he proposed a single multi-level main terminal. At Kansai, as Andreu proposed initially, the domestic departures and arrivals are situated on a middle level, sandwiched between international departures on the top floor and international arrivals on the ground floor. All flights are boarded from lounges on the same immensely long concourse.

The whole airport, not just the 1.7 kilometre long terminal, has already been described as one of the wonders of our time. The island on which it stands apparently ranks with the Great Wall of China (and presumably a few other land reclamation projects) as a man-made artefact that can be identified from space.

Measuring 4.37 by 1.25 kilometres, the island took five years to complete. Osaka's existing Itami Airport, which also served the port of Kobe, was hemmed in by buildings and offered no prospect for growth on such a scale. By contrast a new airport in Osaka Bay could be sited and angled so

that planes could land and take-off over the sea and operate unrestricted for twenty-four hours a day. Steel caissons were sunk to create the perimeter of the island and three mountains were razed to provide the infill of crushed rock. In the event, initial predictions which suggested that the soft clay seabed would settle up to 8 metres with the weight of the infill were exceeded.

Six of Japan's largest construction companies (which have their own in-house architecture departments) were asked to submit proposals for the design of the terminal. Nikken Sekkei's scheme was chosen and sent to a selection of airport authorities around the world for comment. It was at this point that Aéroports de Paris, led by Paul Andreu, came back with a sketch for a wholly new concept. The Kansai International Airport Company was attracted by the potential for very direct transfers between domestic and international flights – without the usual race from one terminal to another with the risk of missing the connection and losing baggage.

Andreu's solution was adopted and the airport company announced an international competition, inviting fifteen practices from around the world to compete on a brief drawn up with the help of Aéroports de Paris. The Renzo Piano Building Workshop, although it had no previous experience

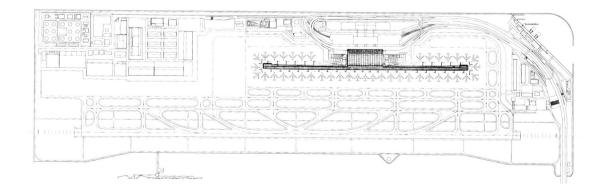

Masterplan

of building airports, had two talented Japanese associates, Noriaki Okabe and Shunji Ishida. Okabe approached Peter Rice of the engineers Ove Arup & Partners (who had worked with Piano on the Pompidou Centre in Paris) and together they convinced Piano to compete. When Piano visited the site with Rice in 1988 he felt that it should be given the character of a natural island with trees along the edge; trees which might invade the terminal. Of all the entrants Piano was the only one to adhere to Andreu's solution.

Piano wrote, 'I believe that structure, especially of an air terminal, should be the diagram of people moving through it.' At Kansai he conceived two valleys full of daylight that were penetrated by nature, one on the landside and one on the airside. Within the two protected environments of the building, the two valleys, in Piano's words, 'echo external nature and become an instinctive destination for passengers moving across the building'. Movement through the building, he adds, must be simple and direct.

Piano produced a stunning model with a sweeping and gleaming metallic roof suggestive of aircraft technology. Long wings extended from the main terminal building to serve forty-two airbridges set in one long straight line. The main body of the terminal has four principal floors with a submerged basement containing baggage handling and plant. The departure hall is at the top, fourth level, served by a high-level access road with a drop-off lane protected by a deep projecting canopy.

Piano was determined to preserve the openness of the departure hall and all the concourses while meeting fire requirements; all the concessions – shops and bars – were set on the third level where they could be doused with sprinklers and closed off behind fire doors.

The second level contains domestic departure. This is also the level of the airbridges and the railway station, which is connected to the terminal by an enclosed bridge running between the upper and lower-level roadways. Immediately below, the ground level (from the airside) contains, first, domestic baggage handling and then the

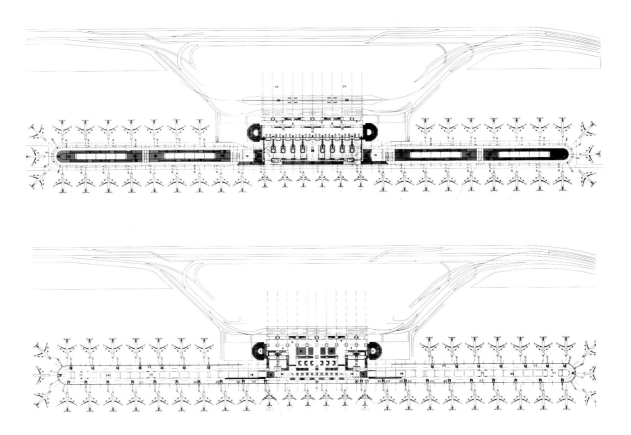

FROM ABOVE: First level plan; second level plan

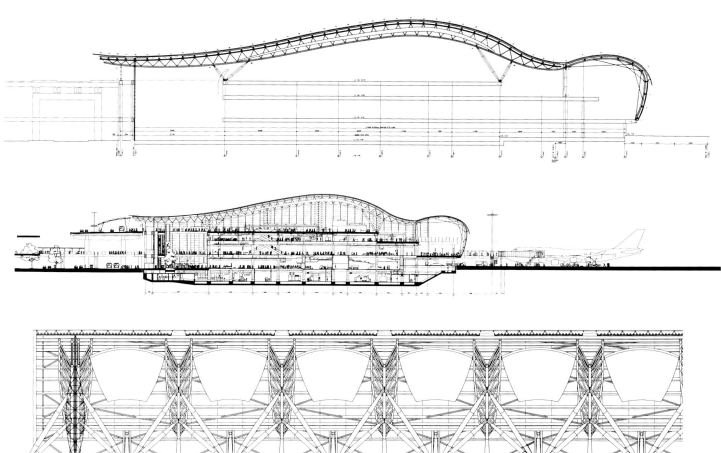

FROM ABOVE: Sections; roof structure

international baggage claim and arrivals lobby. Domestic baggage claim and arrivals are situated on Level 2 domestic departures.

The whole design and layout is intended to be strongly directional. This was an implicit correction of the Stansted terminal, which offers identical views in every direction. (Although orientation at Stansted is clear, the design, if repeated unmodified, could have forfeited good orientation due to the large scale of Kansai.)

The main criticism of the scheme is that the clarity of the design of the landside is obscured by the structures built up against it, notably the elevated road serving departures which is at an unusually high level and overshadows those arriving by train. Piano had intended maximum transparency but cutbacks led to solid walls being introduced at the rail entrance with the unfortunate result that passengers can miss seeing the escalators immediately inside the doors which ascend to international departures and may have to retrace their steps.

From the main terminal building, three-coach shuttle trains depart from the third level and run along the landside of the boarding wings to stations placed midway and at the ends. Escalators descend from the stations to long boarding concourses which lead to departure lounges and airbridges on the second level.

From an early stage, it was clear that the roof structure would be steel, which offered the potential for long spans at an economic price. Arched trusses could provide exhilarating lofty spaces towards the centre, descending towards the edge and so ensuring that the tails of the aircraft would always be visible from the control tower.

Finally, careful provision has been made for maintenance with rails and small trolleys at beam level, providing direct access for cleaning and to all roof equipment, lighting and smoke extractors. The potentially harmful presence of birds is to be controlled by the use of specially trained hawks, artificial robotic hawks and ultrasound.

Piano was conscious that the jury would be viewing his model from above and that the design of the roof was thus critical. The roof is the expression of his belief in the possibility, at the end of the twentieth century, of 'a mature and totally new balance between technology and nature, machine and man, the future and tradition'. So while the steel and glass roof echoes those of the great nineteenth-century termini, in Piano's words it is also reminiscent of 'an aircraft fuselage with the skin peeled off to let in light and to give a glimpse of the underlying construction'. He adds:

> In the wings, at the entrance, light repetitive, braced arches – alternate arches, strutted and supported – remind us of early biplanes, while the pre-stressed cable mullions and the suspended glass facade speak of the technology of today.

The Kansai International Airport Company had envisaged that the winning design would be handed over to Japanese architects and engineers to develop and implement, but Piano insisted that the whole design was based on a close collaboration with Ove Arup & Partners and a consortium was set up, also involving Nikken Sekkei, Aéroports de Paris and Japan Airports Consultants, Inc, to carry through and execute the design. Construction was started on 24 May 1991 but tragically Peter Rice died in October 1992 without seeing completion of the great roof. The airport was inaugurated on 4 September 1994.

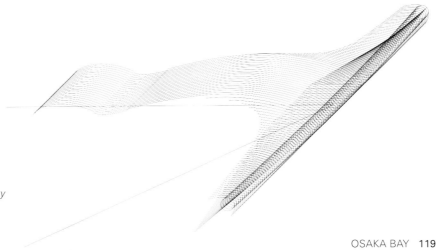

Roof geometry

KUALA LUMPUR INTERNATIONAL AIRPORT

Malaysia

Designed in association with the Malaysian practice, Akitek Jururancang, this airport is planned in the grand manner with a scale and symmetrical perfection that would have pleased the creator of Versailles. In the masterplan, four runways and two central terminals are linked under the apron to four cruciform satellites. The intended completion date is 2020.

The Government of Malaysia initially committed itself to building a world-class new airport that would open in time for the Commonwealth Games in September 1998. The terminal complex is intended to transform Kuala Lumpur International Airport into a major Asian and Pacific hub, competing with Singapore and providing the newest, highest standards for passenger and baggage handling. The first phase consists of a main terminal, a concourse pier with departure gates and a satellite.

Kurokawa compares the terminal to a series of body cells: 'If extra space is needed it can be achieved by simple repetition of the basic module.' Along the outside edges the roof is cantilevered forward, like a peaked cap, to shade the glass beneath. This is inclined from the top at an angle of fifteen degrees to reduce heat gain.

Architecturally, the airport sets out to offer more than the latest in international high-tech, providing a distinctly Malaysian atmosphere that will create a favourable first impression of the country. This is achieved by billowing roofs and abundant natural light, with panoramic windows providing views of lush vegetation around the main concourses.

Model view

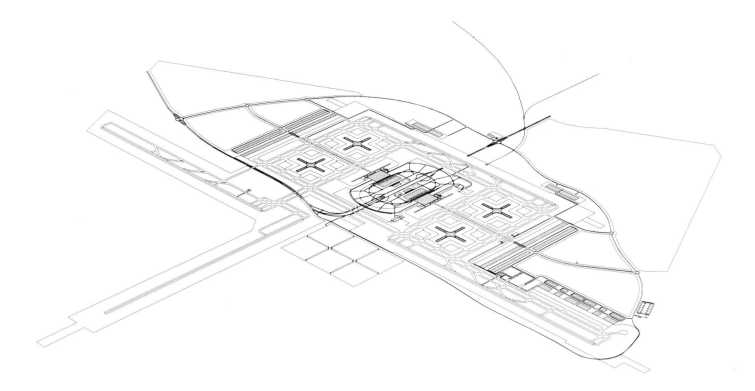

Axonometric

Kurokawa won the commission in a competition against considerable odds. The site for the complex, which he describes as 'a symbiosis of nature and high-tech', encompasses a vast area (more than 10 kilometres square). This was previously covered by a palm oil plantation.

The swooping lines of the roof create a tent-like image, reinforcing the outdoor feel of what is inevitably an enclosed building constructed to meet stringent security requirements. The departures area is at the top on Level 5, the international concourse is on Level 4, and the arrivals area is situated on Level 3. All provide generous space for passengers, with ample provision for shops, bars and cafes.

Departure gates open off a long concourse in front of the terminal, looking out towards the runways. Further gates are provided along the arms of the satellite which has below-ground connections with the main terminal. The cross plan minimises walking distances.

In the centre of the satellite there is a glazed circular courtyards planted with small forest trees. These verdant courtyard is approached on the way to taking the train to the main terminal. Kurokawa explains:

> The forest is a symbol for Malaysia, so we determined that the first impression for passengers as they disembark should be of a rainforest.

The shells of the main terminal roof are compared by Kurokawa to the domes of Islamic architecture. The underside is slatted in wood, a conscious tribute to Malaysia's importance as a long-standing centre of sustainable timber production. It is designed in such a way that all the timbers run straight, making the most economical use of the wood. Glass roof-slits, the shape of laurel leaves, allow sunlight to penetrate the roof, but the overall effect is of cooling shade.

The external roof finish is in steel, bake-painted like an automobile, comments Kurokawa. The concrete columns, clad in Italian granite, have the cone-shape proportions of a Dalek robot. They contain the ventilation system, avoiding the need to place cooling systems on the roof. To emphasise the tactile perfection of the terminal, the wooden roof is not inset with light fittings. By contrast, in the long concourse opening directly off the departures hall, ceiling spots are placed randomly in the ceiling to create the effect of a starlit sky. Below, highly polished granite floors provide a near mirror reflection of the structure above.

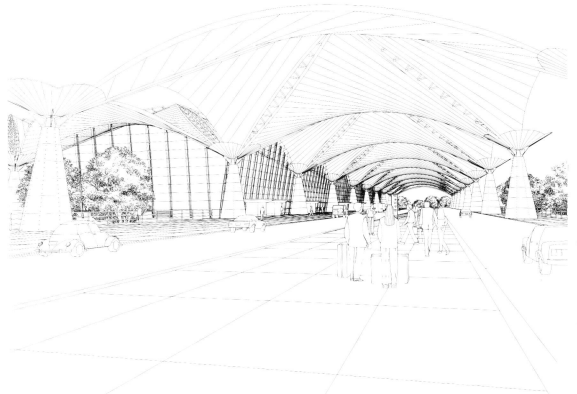

Perspective

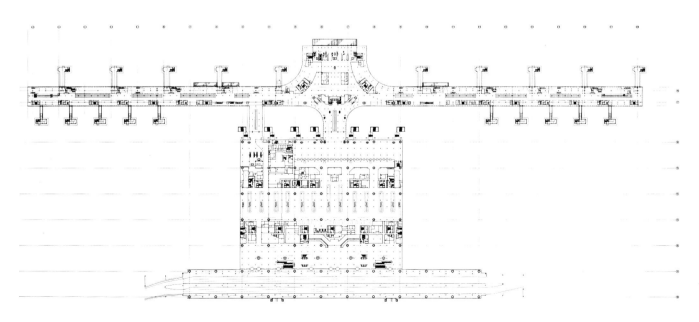

Third floor plan

Section

Elevation

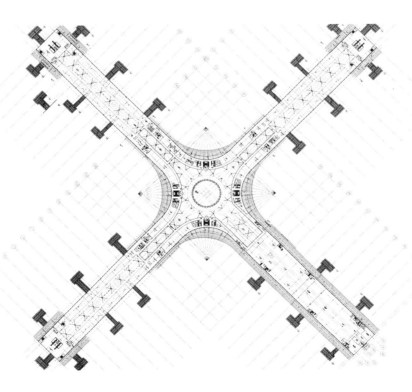

Plan of satellite, mezzanine level

Section of satellite

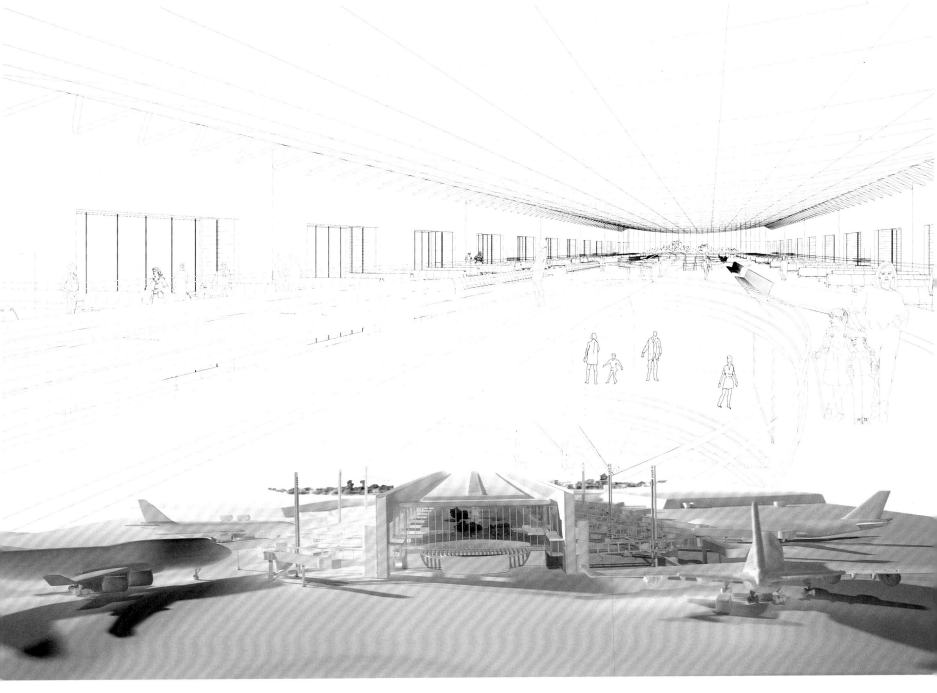

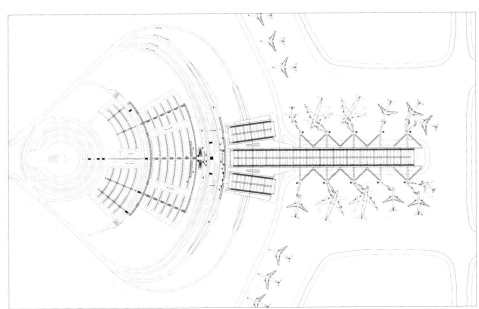

FROM ABOVE: Perspective; model; site plan; OPPOSITE, FROM ABOVE: Airside elevation; west elevation

LARNACA AIRPORT, NEW TERMINAL

Cyprus

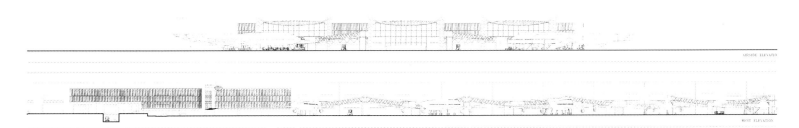

The Cyprus Government has ambitious plans to make Larnaca a major hub for the eastern Mediterranean. Cyprus Airways, based at the airport, will be the main beneficiary. The master-plan, approved in 1994 by the Communications Minister, provides for a new terminal and new runway. From three proposals, the government chose that of a French-led consortium consisting of Aéroports de Paris (led by Paul Andreu) and Sofréavia, J & A Philippou and Forum Architects.

The plans provide for completely new passenger and cargo terminals to the west of the existing facilities and for a 500-metre extension to the runway, giving it a total length of 3,500 metres. As is characteristic of Andreu's work, the whole layout is marshalled along strict symmetrical lines, achieving mirror symmetry wherever possible. This applies most obviously to the terminal and surrounding aircraft stands and also to the remote stands. Further out, the cargo centre is balanced by the administration and service area where a new control tower is positioned at one end.

The new terminal consists of three large halls set along a gently curving approach road. In response to the curve, the three halls are not exactly parallel but fan outward like the spokes of a wheel, with office space inserted in between. The side halls measure 100 by 45 metres while the central hall is prolonged into a 430-metre-long concourse pier. The arrivals area is situated below with departures above. The total surface area is 75,200 square metres.

A Mediterranean character is conveyed by the solid walls, which are pierced by large arches and penetrated by filtered light from the roof. Large zig-zag trusses are employed to create wide column-free spans. Openness is maintained in the long pier, which has two passenger levels for arrivals and departures. Here, the upper departure levels are set back from the outer wall like a balcony to reinforce the sense of openness. The pier is conceived as a single uninterrupted space with seating placed continuously along the windows. At regular intervals, central oval balconies provide a view of the floor below. These are crossed by the moving walkways which will speed passengers to the more distant gates. At the end of the pier a larger oval balcony opens on to a lushly planted double-height garden.

The arrangement of the airbridges is unusually complex with three passageways linked to a circular node. These connect alternately with the departures and arrivals levels. From the nodes, one of two telescopic arms moves out to lock on to the aircraft door. Both arms meet jumbo-size aircraft which have two doors at the front.

On the arrivals level of the pier, additional moving walkways speed passengers to a broad immigration hall which widens out into a large baggage reclaim area. Beyond, the hall's designated meeting area opens into a series of well planted gardens with the pick-up points and car parks beyond.

According to the Cypriot Communications Minister, in 1995 the total investment was planned at CYP 232 million (approximately $116 million) and completion was scheduled for 2001.

South elevation

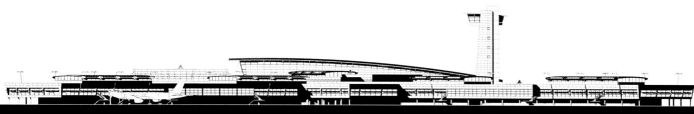

East elevation

McCARRAN AIRPORT, SATELLITE D
Las Vegas, Nevada, US

Like airports all over the USA, Las Vegas is expanding. A new island satellite is being constructed with forty-eight gates on an X-plan: a configuration that combines the maximum number of airbridges with the shortest walking distances. The first phase, with twenty-six gates, consists of two arms of the X, forming a V, and comprises 41,800 square metres.

An automatic transit system will connect the satellite beneath the aprons with the main terminal with an impressive time of ninety seconds for the one kilometre journey. The above-ground component of the satellite consists of one level of masonry surmounted by a structure of steel columns and beams, with abundant windows and metal cladding. Ground level contains operational space, and the first upper level (Level 2) contains the passenger concourse. As the satellite is used purely for domestic flights, there are no customs or immigration check points and no need for separation of departing and arriving passengers (international passengers land at Terminal 2). Four baggage claim carousels are housed in the main terminal for arriving passengers to pick up their baggage.

As this is Las Vegas, the new satellite is visually spectacular, as colourful, brash and vibrant as the city's famous Strip. Neon light is in abundance: white neon on the waving ceiling and dozens of flashing coloured neon signs. Artificial palm trees extend to a height of 12 metres.

Transparent walls (using glass supplied by Pilkington's) provide views of the runway, mountains and, just a few kilometres away, The Strip everyone has come to see. Perforated sunshades, held in place by cables, protect the glass from outside temperatures which can rise to 50°C.

The satellite has a series of themed shopping galleries – an Airstrip to match the downtown strip, complete with ranks of slot machines; an Area 51, evoking space-ships and aliens in the Nevada Desert; Lake Tahoe for the eco-friendly holidaymaker; and the Entertainer, based on Las Vegas shows. Ruby's Diner and the Prickly Pear are among restaurants with a local theme.

There is also an array of public art, including sixteen large children's murals contributed by pupils in different cities – London was one of the winners with a 4 x 5 metre panel of Buckingham Palace, the Guards and Big Ben. The floor of the Rotunda is a terrazzo flightmap of the Las Vegas area. There are large concrete statues of desert animals, such as the horny toad (a local lizard), a snake and a scorpion. Columns resemble the tail-fins of planes, while hanging light fixtures evoke flight in the form of wings and aero-engines.

The $176 million new satellite was commissioned by the airport owner, Clark County Department of Aviation, and serves TWA, American Airlines, and Northwest, United and Delta airlines. The design process commenced in December 1994 and was finalised in February 1996 with construction beginning in July of that year. Opening of the first phase was scheduled for 1998, and it is hoped that the two further arms of the satellite will be constructed over the next three years.

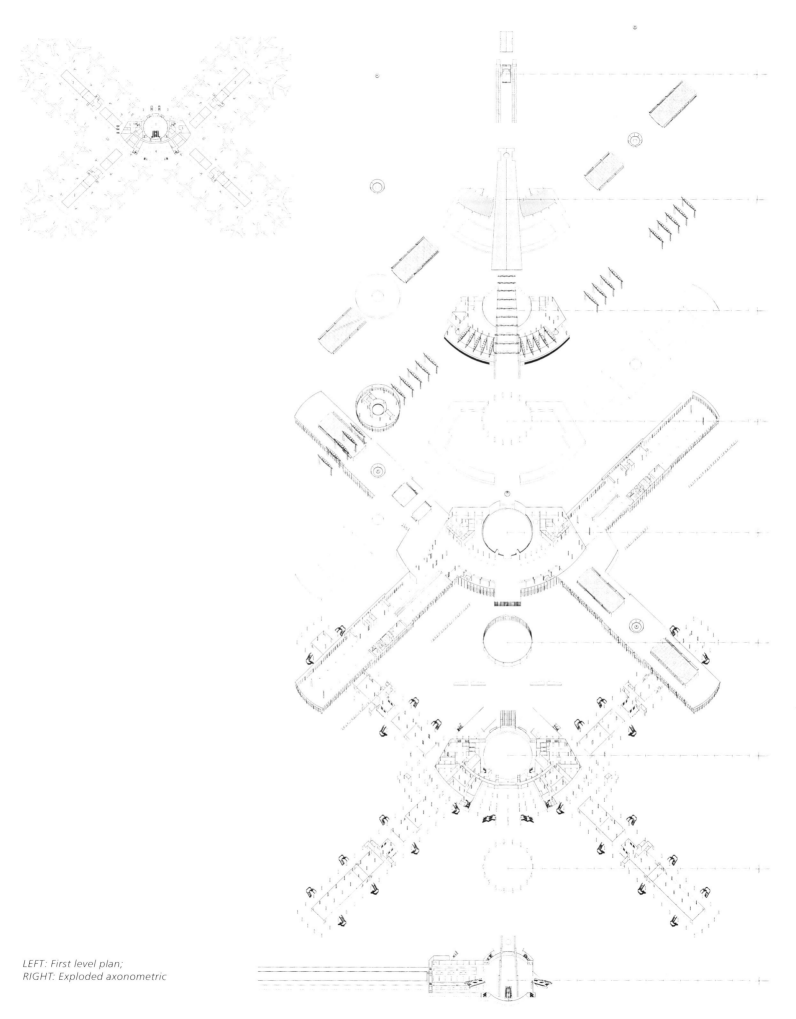

LEFT: First level plan;
RIGHT: Exploded axonometric

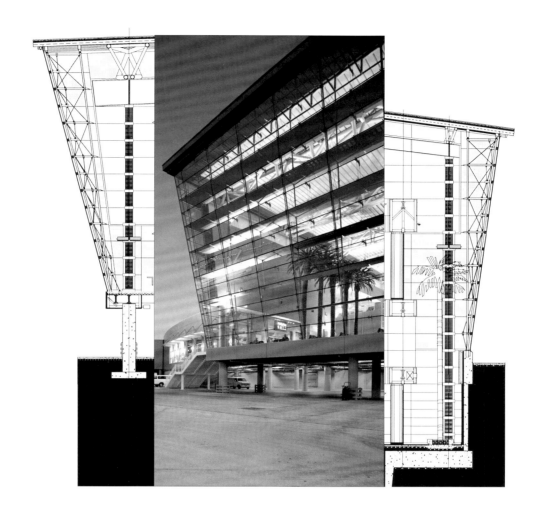

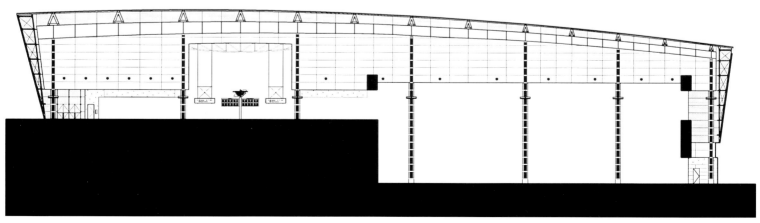

Sections

LILLE AIRPORT, PASSENGER TERMINAL
Lille-Lesquin, France

In the wake of the Channel Tunnel, Lille has become a rail junction of major importance, with numerous Eurostar trains between London and both Paris and Brussels stopping at a handsome new station designed by the great engineer Peter Rice. Inevitably, the airport had to be modern too and the design chosen is a fashionable and striking essay in Deconstruction. The airport is situated ten minutes from the city centre and is at the hub of motorways linking Brussels, London and Paris. An SNCF station serves the airport and 700 carparking spaces are provided on two levels.

The new terminal, which opened in May 1996, was commissioned by the Lille/Roubaix Tourcoing Chamber of Commerce and Industry. It offers splintered forms, trapezoidal spaces, sharp angles and leaning walls. 'It symbolises the new dynamism of a town that turns determinedly towards the twenty-first century,' remarks Dennis Sloan. The magazine *Building* commented, 'You can easily spot the long, low, silver fuselage, the high triangular tailplane and a nose as sharply pointed as Concorde's,' adding that, 'as well as an airplane soaring in flight, it can bring to mind a crash-landing of a jumbo jet'. But in Lille, which boasts a Congress Hall by Rem Koolhaus and a shopping centre by Jean Nouvel, such innovation in design is less surprising than it might be among more conventional surroundings.

With the main departure level situated 6 metres above ground, the terminal is a major landmark from the motorway. Diagonal, dagger-like shapes constantly attract the eye. The metal canopy over the departure drop-off point has the double slope of a Mansard roof. Instead of vertical columns, the girders are formed in a V. The outer girders are inclined forward to meet narrow triangular blades which support the canopy roof. Sloan rejects Deconstructionist associations:

> Personally I see it as more a sort of porcupine style. The building is enlivened by protrusions and glass projections jutting out, almost at random, in all directions.'

For all its wilful asymmetry, the plan layout of the building is relatively straightforward. As at Norman Foster's Stansted Airport, the passenger facilities are housed largely in the upper hall, with service areas and offices arranged on the lower levels. Moveable screens are used to create a flexible interior.

Sloan described the objective of airport design to the magazine *L'Arca* as fulfilling the desire to

> simply get on and off the plane as quickly as possible. So, no corridors, no waiting for the luggage. On top of this and just for fun, one wants to see the planes take off and land.

The cost of construction of the terminal itself was 150 million FF, with a further 81 million FF for associated works, mainly to the aprons. Finance was provided variously by the state, the EU, the region, the Department du Nord, greater Lille, the City, and the Chamber of Commerce and Airport.

Between winning the competition in March 1991 and starting construction in 1994, Dennis Sloan was obliged to reduce costs by thirty per cent. This was done largely by care in choosing materials – colour-coated steel rather than aluminium cladding; industrial crinkly tin for the undercroft; single-membrane PVC roof covering rather than zinc; terrazzo instead of marble floors; and perforated steel panels for the ceilings. Atelier Sloan sought specialist advice from the aviation consultancy Sofréavia. The project managers were Bovis Construction.

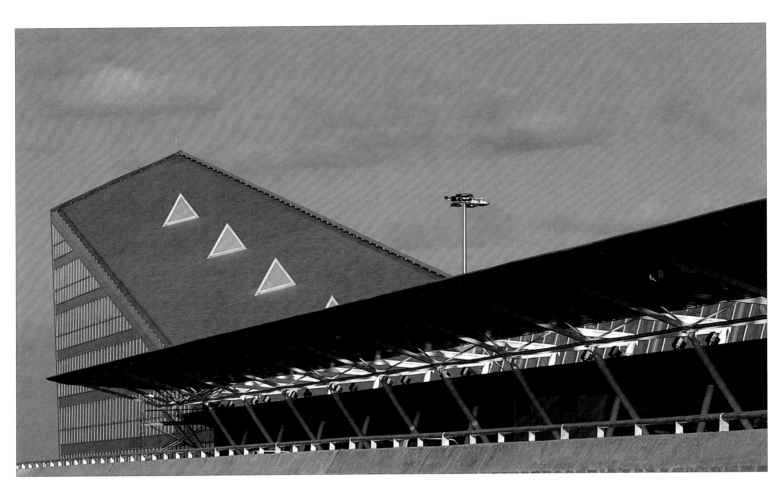

FROM ABOVE: South elevation; west elevation; east elevation; north elevation

Computer-generated view of exterior

LONDON HEATHROW AIRPORT, TERMINAL 5
United Kingdom

London Heathrow ranks as the world's busiest international airport and existing terminals are inadequate to meet predicted growth. Whether such growth should occur is contested fiercely by many West London residents, but the design for the new terminal is a determined attempt to replace the piecemeal growth of the airport with an ordered layout that can be extended in the future. The decision to proceed is dependent on the outcome of a public inquiry that has already, at the time of writing, run for three years.

The proposed location is at the western end of the present airport, between the runways, on the site of the Perry Oaks sludge works. The plans allow for a new road link on to the M25 motorway, and direct rail access to the centre of London via the Paddington–Heathrow Express link (with a fifteen-minute journey time) and the Piccadilly tube line which runs beneath the city.

The Rogers partnership interpreted the brief as requiring a new gateway to the UK, 'a landmark building celebrating the magic and excitement of travel' seeking to ensure 'a great sense of occasion' as people moved through the terminal and to create an ambience of calm and visual clarity.

The design process has focused on the creation of a multi-storey terminal through which abundant daylight descends to the lowest level. The new terminal measures 400 by 250 metres with a roof rising to 40 metres in the centre, making it the highest terminal building in the UK. The architects have used a wave form to soften its bulk and the roof is shown oversailing the glass walls in all directions – over the departure drop-off by a staggering 25 metres. Its new departure concourse is a full 20 metres above ground level.

John Young, the partner in charge at the Rogers office, explains, 'We have lowered the roof on both landside and airside, and the projections give it an impression of floating.' The intention is that from the moment travellers leave the M25 the roof will be visible. Great pains are being taken to ensure that the inevitable car parks in front do not destroy or obscure its lines. These will be stepped up in layers and luxuriantly planted. According to Young, adjoining buildings such as a hotel and offices will rise no higher than the departures forecourt in order to 'accentuate the impression of a light and airy pavilion straddling a plateau of landscaping.'

Passengers arriving by tube or train will immediately see the full height of the building as they emerge at the bottom of a deep atrium surrounded by tiers of balconies and crossed by bridges, a setting creating a dramatic sense of anticipation as they alight in the very heart of the terminal. Escalators will provide an impressive, animated ascent equivalent to the grand staircase halls of public buildings in earlier centuries.

The roof will be carried by a series of steel supports, creating a hall continuously open to the roof at departure level, with bands of glass admitting daylight from one end to the other. As Young explains, a steel structure also reduces the amount of aggregates used in both the building and the foundations. He adds:

> From the early days of the design, one of my guiding principles has been to design a contemporary equivalent to the great nineteenth-century railway stations, heroic structures where the architecture enriched the travelling experience through a sense of space and the quality of light within.

Arrivals level will be approximately 10 metres above ground level. A very large number of passengers, perhaps fifty per cent, will simply transfer from one flight to another. Baggage handling is accommodated at ground level.

Computer-generated views of interior and site

This area requires ceiling heights of 8 metres. Roof spans can be 36 metres, but the roofs are merely envelopes – all mechanical services will come from below.

Future expansion is provided for in two parallel satellites (Atlanta style) with airside departure lounges. These will be connected to Terminal 5 by walkways under the aprons. The aim is to create a family of roof structures with visual consistency and harmony. Roofs will be low at the edges, rising to let light into a central atrium. Young has also designed a new tower or Visual Control Room (VCR) for the new terminal.

The British Airports Authority expects the new terminal to cost some £800 million. One third of the cost will be accounted for by the baggage system, which, according to the engineer Chris Wise of Ove Arup & Partners, 'is more significant than the cladding or the structure. It could cater for thirty million passengers a year.' He comments, 'Terminal 5 will shift the building industry and improve the way buildings are designed.

LONDON HEATHROW AIRPORT, EUROPIER
United Kingdom

London Heathrow comprises a jumble of buildings displaying correspondingly varied standards of architecture. Elegant in both conception and execution, the Europier (attached to Terminal 1) is a perfect illustration of the startling impact of excellence in design, even amid such unpromising surroundings. Both outside and in, the Europier stands out for its clean lines, handsome proportions, spaciousness and attention to detail. Moreover, the sense of openness and abundance of light are appreciated in an airport which in many places has the claustrophobic qualities of a maze.

Precisely because the whole length of the concourse is open to view – without being so long that the travellers wonder whether they will ever reach that distant gate – it has an instantly soothing effect. Fears of missing the flight fall away. Travellers can see the plane and, equally, the departure gate staff can see any last passengers coming towards them.

The sense of calm is enhanced by the breadth of the central concourse – wide enough to ensure the passage ahead is never likely to be blocked. The axiality is emphasised by the pair of ceiling ducts running the length of the pier – this is a view which should never be blocked by a kiosk or check-in desk. Running the length of the concourse there is abundant seating which is generously spaced so passengers can manoeuvre effortlessly past each other even with their trollies; the seating is also low, eliminating any possible sense of clutter.

The sense of freedom is increased by the fact that passengers are not corralled into holdrooms at departure gates. If their flight is full, they can simply sit a few yards further away, eliminating the need to search for the last spare seat.

Visual monotony is avoided by a subtle asymmetry, which provides an effective counterpoint to the strong axiality. On one side, an upper gallery has been introduced, its glass walls maintaining the sense of transparency. On the other, floor-to-ceiling glass provides a glorious sense of openness and light. The panes are large and the mullions the slenderest forms possible. They are stiffened by diagonal ties springing from the columns which are themselves intentionally slender and widely spaced. The sense of loftiness is increased by the way the columns branch out at their apex to support the roof at four points.

The pier is conceived as a repeating module, using the maximum number of standardised industrial components – glazing, cladding, ceiling panels and roofing. Measuring 280 metres long, the £30 million Europier is the last main phase of a £150 million redevelopment of Heathrow's Terminal 1, which includes a new international departures lounge and a new Flight Connections Centre for passengers transferring from one flight to another. The Europier provides ten gates serving ten new aircraft stands. There is seating for 1,130 passengers and 600 square metres of space for retailing and catering outlets.

The building incorporates 4,000 square metres of glass and 1,600 tonnes of steel. Construction began in July 1994 and the building became operational on 4 December 1995. Terminal 1 at Heathrow now handles twenty-two million passengers a year and is destined to be Europe's fifth busiest airport in its own right.

The Flight Connections Centre opened in December 1994 and contains showers, a slumber zone and children's play area. The international departures lounge, which opened in October 1995, includes considerable additional seating and shopping facilities and a 5.5-metre-wide aquarium. Both these buildings were designed by the Richard Rogers Partnership.

Model of Europier and new passenger link to Terminal 1

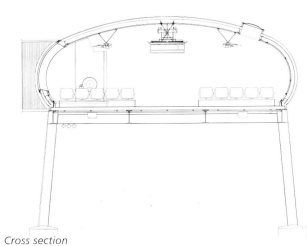

Cross section

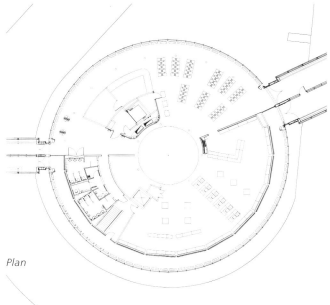

Plan

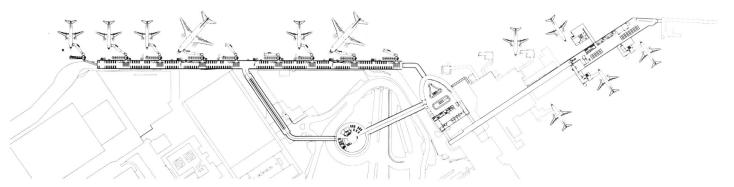

Plan of overall development

LONDON HEATHROW AIRPORT, PIER 4A

United Kingdom

There is a special appeal in what the French call *architecture parlante* – architecture which speaks its purpose. For Heathrow's Pier 4A, completed in 1993, the architects intriguingly developed a whole vocabulary of forms and details which speak of aircraft and flight. The elevated walkways, elliptical in section, resemble long sections of fuselage. The oval windows are like aircraft windows and the suspended light fittings resemble the leading edge of an aircraft wing or fin. All this serves to give a very low budget building a distinct and stylish appearance, using materials more akin to aircraft construction than traditional forms of building.

The brief was to provide a new weather protected walk-on pier to serve nine remote 'November' stands to the west of Terminal 1. The new gates served three groups of domestic or quasi-domestic flights, which nonetheless required separation – domestic flights within England and Scotland; flights to Belfast; and flights within the so-called Common Travel Area, here represented by the Republic of Ireland and the Channel Islands. Passengers travelling within the CTA do not need passports, but passengers from the Channel Islands (which are not in the EC and Irish Republic) do need customs clearance and with this goes the opportunity for outbound passengers to purchase duty-free. The CTA passengers, therefore, have separate routes to a segregated series of gates. In all, there are nine gates for CTA passengers and four for domestic flights.

Before Pier 4A was built, passengers were often faced with lengthy coach-rides to and from the aircraft, something which can still happen if an inbound aircraft is continuing to a European destination and is thus directed to a gate at the far end of Terminal 1.

The new pier had to be built over an existing airside road while other elements such as the CTA lounge, the baggage hall reclaim and ancillary accommodation had to be integrated into a web of roads and existing structures. Headroom had to be maintained over airport roads and sight lines and radar waves considered. The budget was based on an economic life of just nine years as future plans involved the realignment of the taxiway to accommodate larger aircraft.

All public areas are therefore elevated 6 metres above ground. The objective was to produce a structure with minimum height between floor and roof, which could also be built extremely quickly. The solution was to use a series of simple steel portal frames spanning the road, with steel beams spanning from portal to portal and carrying a concrete floor. The concrete floor supports a series of elliptical steel hoops set 2.4 metres apart and forming the basic frame for the cladding.

Silver PVF2 coated British Alcan Sinusoidal aluminium sheet (profile S20) was chosen for the external cladding and internal lining of the hoop structure. Profile aluminium was chosen as the most cost-effective solution to the curved geometry. Sheets used for the tight curves had to be specially pre-formed; the gentler curves could be covered by standard sheeting. A smaller profiled sheeting was used to clad the fixed airbridge links. Aluminium was also used extensively in the internal fittings, for example the lighting booms and the low-level chequer-plate protection.

Arriving passengers from the Republic of Ireland and the Channel Islands have their own dedicated link through the Baggage Reclaim Hall and Customs. With the adjacent domestic Pier 4, Pier 4A handles some ten million passengers per year. The value of the contract was £25 million.

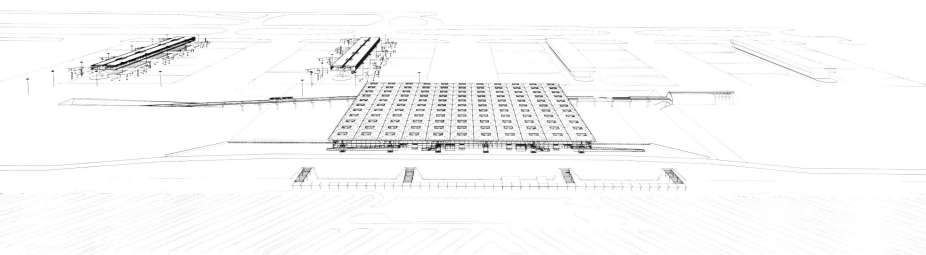

Perspective

LONDON STANSTED AIRPORT
United Kingdom

Sir Norman Foster's Stansted Airport, commissioned in 1981 and opened a decade later, changed the direction of terminal design. To illustrate his design concept, Foster used to begin presentations on Stansted with a photograph of Atlanta Airport in the 1920s, depicting a plain shed with a car on one side and a plane on the other. 'I want to return to the simplicity of early air travel,' he would say.

His aim at Stansted is that passengers should immediately grasp where they are going and always be able to see their path ahead, without the constant changes of level and direction that make so many airports baffling and exhausting to use. He therefore adopted the simple arrangement of placing all passenger facilities on one floor in a huge open hall measuring 200 metres across. Even before the visitor or passenger is through the doors they can catch a glimpse of an aircraft soaring aloft.

The essence of the new terminal is that it is open, light and airy. An abundance of daylight, Foster believes, makes for a much more relaxing and less claustrophobic atmosphere. As terminals have become deeper in plan, so natural lighting has been restricted to the edges. At Stansted it pours in through the roof the length and breadth of the building. This is in marked contrast to the roofs of most airport terminals which, says Foster, are about 'pirouetting vast quantities of mechanical equipment in the air'. His view is that a roof is about two things only – admitting light and keeping out water.

The solution at Stansted is to house all services below the main passenger level, where there is direct ground access for vehicles and service engineers. This is facilitated by a slight fall in the ground.. The higher ground level at the entrance has simply been extended towards the apron as a vast extruded platform.

For those arriving by car, parking is provided entirely at grade one level. Trolleys are available so that passengers can push their luggage up to the departure hall via a broad ramp. The one drawback is that for those returning a hire car, particularly if they are in a hurry, the drop-off point is several hundred yards from the terminal.

Inside, Foster's organising principle is to place departures on the left and arrivals on the right – both on the same level. The aim is that, as far as possible, every one moves in one direction, through check-in, security, passport control to the departure lounge with duty free shopping; and back through immigration, baggage collection and customs.

To avoid long walks past numerous departure gates, a shuttle train transports passengers from the main departure lounge to many of the gates. However, some charter airlines inevitably insist on cheap stands far across the apron which can only be reached by bus.

When Foster received the commission for Stansted from the British Airports Authority the overriding stipulation was that the building should be twenty per cent cheaper – on a square footage basis – than any recently completed terminal. Foster's creative drive is to push constantly for the simplest most elemental solution. Repetition and standardisation are not anathema to him; rather, they are the key to the most efficient, practical and economic solution.

The vast airy space over the concourse is supported by 'trees' – towers of girders which branch out to support the 18-metre-square roof panels. So slender are they in relation to the space as a whole that they give the impression not of holding the roof up, but of preventing it from floating away. This impression is reinforced by the light lattice-dome panels which look as if they are billowing upwards.

Traditionally, architecture is about mass as much as space, using walls to create a sense of enclosure. At Stansted, Foster exploits the modernistic ideal, that architecture is about space and light, by eliminating solid walls altogether, both inside and out. The outer cladding of the concourse is floor-to-ceiling glass. The internal partitions were to rise no higher than the base of the trees. Foster wanted to maximise transparency by using clear glass screens, but for security reasons customs officers would not accept this.

Stansted was under construction just as new EC regulations were due for introduction in 1992 to ease travel between member countries. Hence, Foster was faced with the possibility that the layout of immigration facilities would be changed almost as soon as the terminal was complete. This meant providing for rapid changes of cabling. To do this a floor independent of the trees was designed, made in giant waffle sections with panels that can be changed at will.

Foster believes that colour in buildings, as in nature, should serve a purpose, and not simply act as decoration. The main surfaces are all low-key – 'neutral' is the word he uses. The floors are of grey Sardinian granite; the walls are glass from floor to ceiling. In contrast, bright colours are used to attract the eye to information.

The vast service area below the passenger concourse has been designed to ensure that cables and ducts running in one direction do not have to duck under those running across. The same sophisticated engineering techniques operate in the roof. Usually, a large expanse of roof requires valley gutters with pipes descending down internal columns, with the result that when a burst pipe occurs this can cause havoc, especially so close to sensitive cabling. At Stansted, Foster has used a patent Finnish system, new to the UK, which syphons the water off the roof horizontally. Normally, air and water mix freely in the rainwater pipes. This system restricts the amount of air that enters and syphonic pressure is created in the down-pipes which telescope towards the bottom, sucking the water off the whole width of the roof.

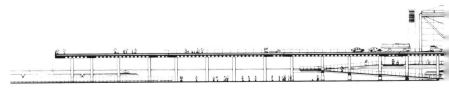

Elevation

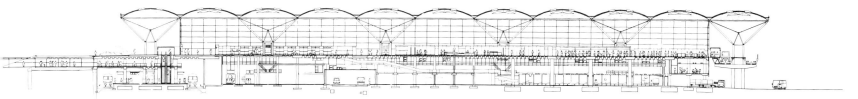

Section

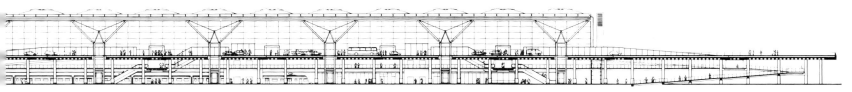

OPPOSITE, FROM ABOVE: Plan of main terminal concourse; masterplan

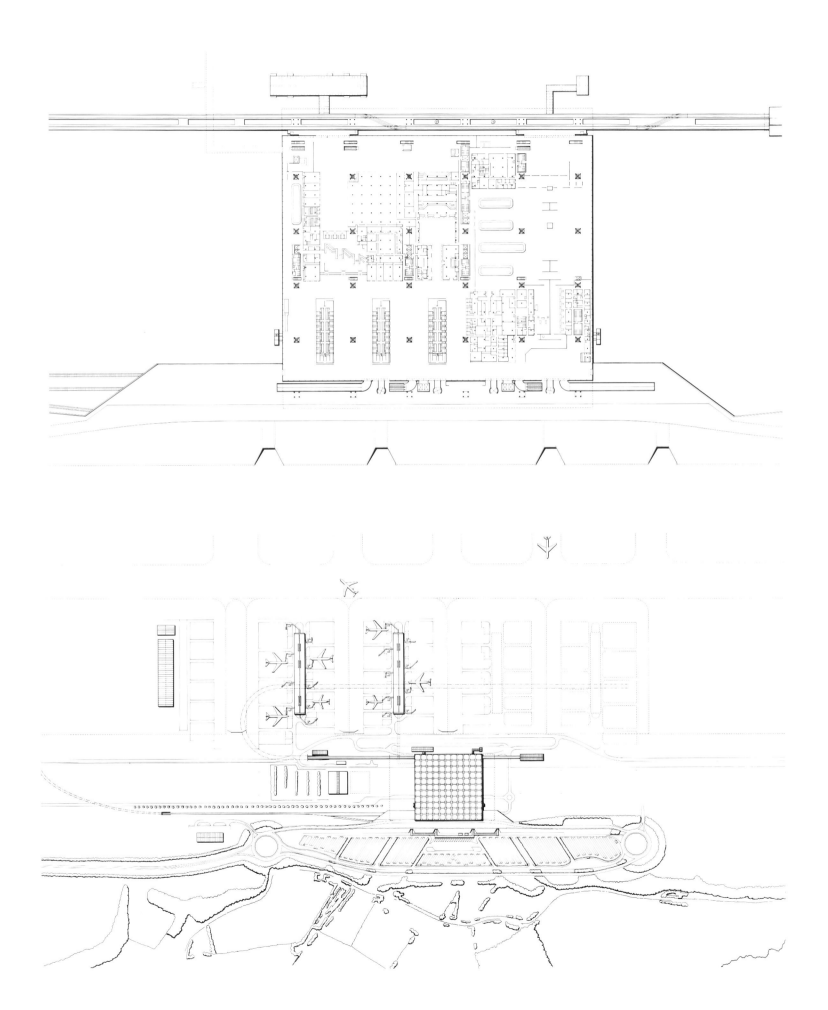

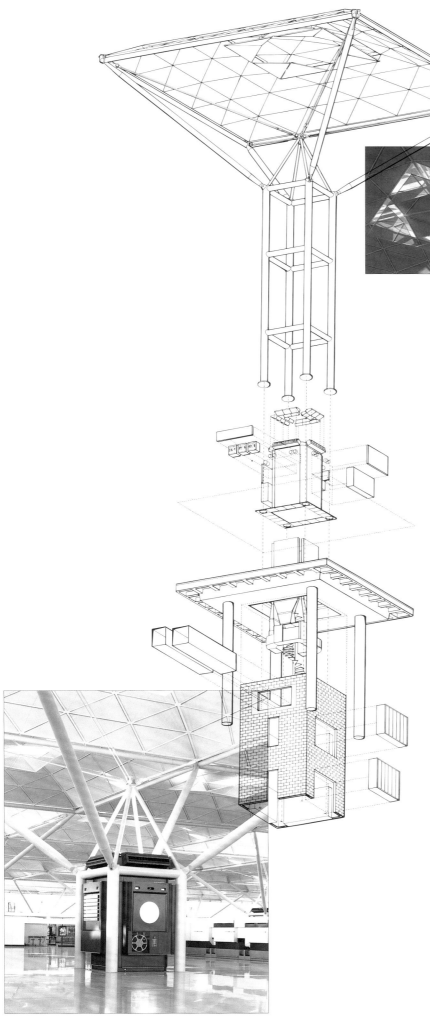

Foster's trees hold up a vast grid of primary beams. Once these were in position individual roof sections could be craned into place without the need for scaffolding. Foster likes to turn up the Charles Eames chairs in his office revealing the birdcage support below and say, 'here you have Stansted'. The trees also contain both the intake and the outlet for the air-conditioning as well as uplighters which dramatically illuminate the interior at night.

Transport is equally efficient and streamlined. The new railway station which links Stansted with London's Liverpool Street Station by half-hourly trains has also been designed by the Foster office. In keeping with the airport itself, the lofty station roof is supported on slender concrete columns, and passengers coming from the car park cross the station on open bridges.

Axonometric of tree and services pod

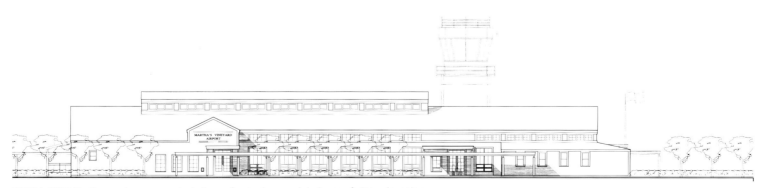

FROM ABOVE: Computer-generated view of exterior; aerial views of site; elevation

MARTHA'S VINEYARD AIRPORT, NEW TERMINAL

Massachusetts, US

Here is a small airport that bucks the trend. While most airports look ever more international, this facility is designed as an offshoot of the earth on which it stands – the shallow pitch of the roofs, the cedar-shingle hung walls and the smart white window trim all speak of New England tradition.

Martha's Vineyard is one of the most attractive and jealously preserved islands along the northeast US coast. As visitors have steadily increased, the existing terminal, a Second World War naval airbase complex, has become inadequate.

The new $8 million 1,630-square-metre terminal, due to open in 1999, takes its proportions, material and colouring from the unadorned summer cabins on the shore. Simple white edging is used to outline the roof and the angles of the control tower. Inside, the architects make a virtue of natural materials, exposing the wooden roof, which is braced with metal rods to achieve added openness and lightness, and extending the roof timbers scissor-fashion to create a raised rooflight.

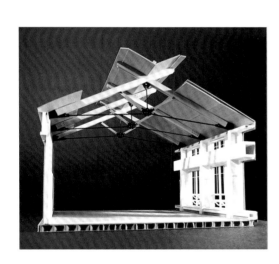

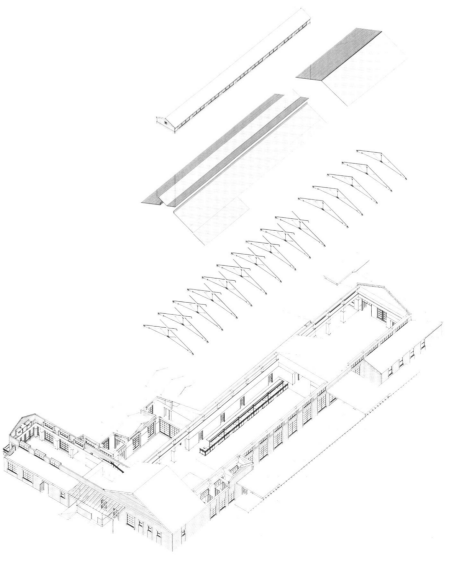

LEFT: Model section; RIGHT: Axonometric

VON BUSSE & PARTNERS
MUNICH AIRPORT, PASSENGER TERMINAL
Germany

Munich Airport, which was begun in 1985 and formally inaugurated on 17 May 1992, is the embodiment of the complete and harmoniously planned new airport. Everything is new – roads, runways, buildings and landscaping. The whole concept has the symmetry, hierarchy and orderliness of a neo-classical town planned by an Enlightenment prince. Although eclectic (involving a variety of design firms), the architecture has a 'family' likeness, creating the impression of an ideal settlement not only planned as a unified entity but executed in such a short space of time that nothing is discordant.

The story is well set out in a commemorative volume, *Munich Airport: Landscape Visual Design Architecture* published in May 1992. Munich is the second major transport hub in central Europe after Frankfurt. The new terminal is designed to handle fifteen million passengers a year, with the possibility of a second terminal at a later date.

The debate on whether and where to build a new airport began in the 1970s. The site chosen was the Erdinger Moor, a large stretch of former moorland to the north of the city. The land, used previously for hunting and peat extraction, had been drained in the 1920s following the construction of the Middle Isar Canal. Used originally for grazing, it had been drained to the point where intensive arable farming became possible. The land was flat and arranged in rectangular strips aligned along the drainage ditches.

The landscaping plan for the airport involves maintaining large areas as meadows, mown just twice a year. New earthworks such as ditches, ramps and knolls are left as recognisably man-made features. Stands of wood are planted as clearly ordered formations or as isolated trees, the species found in the surrounding landscape. There is no attempt to mask buildings with planting; instead they are left open to view.

In architectural terms, debate centred on whether a typical Munich or Bavarian airport could be created, and whether a standardised design should be established for all the new buildings – be they cargo handling facilities, hangars, administrative blocks or emergency services.

The conclusions were to equate a Bavarian approach, not with a particular style or form, but with a high degree of quality in both form and function 'in a manner pleasing to the public'. Given the size of the site and the distances between buildings, it was also agreed there should be a diversity of architectural signatures. The crucial guidelines were:

- to ensure road and rail access from east and west;
- to provide a railway station forming an integral part of the terminal;
- to allow the landscape to be an integral part of the development;
- to create openness, generous expanse and logical order to assure easy orientation;
- to space individual zones to allow for future expansion without mutual encroachment, such expansion to be carried out according to the orderly principles of the original layout;
- to characterise buildings, especially passenger facilities, by openness, transparency and a sense of scale;
- to avoid creating canyon-like streets and stacked roads;
- to ensure that modular design allows for future extension in building block fashion.

Recognising the need to establish common denominators, Otl Aicher and Eberhard Stauss presented the overall visual design concept with the theme of unity in diversity. The basic precept was that all buildings should reflect the rational,

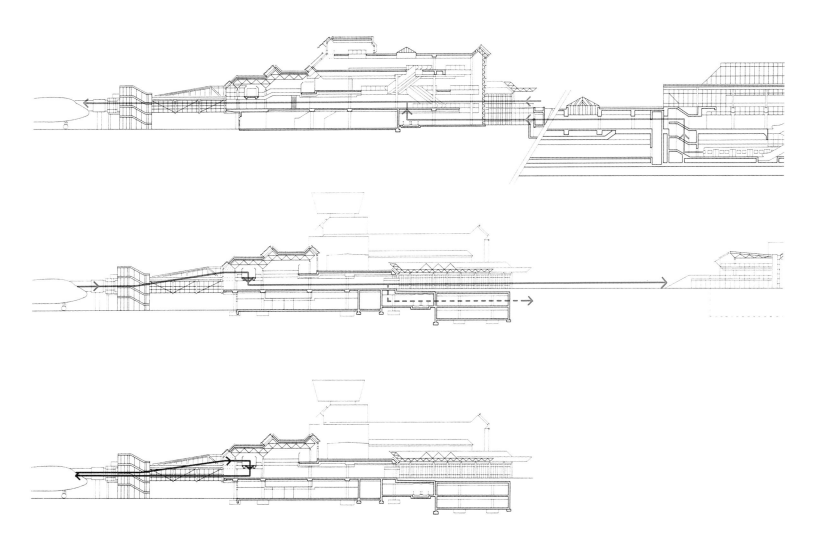

FROM ABOVE: Departure, arrival and transfer sections

functionalist, technically organised principles of modern architecture.

Four major architectural competitions set the framework. The first, for the passenger terminal, was limited to twelve invited participants. At the time, it was claimed that the detailed spatial and structural stipulations of the brief would make the competition a token event limiting the architects to designing facades. In fact, the solutions were very different and there was a hard fought second round between Meinhard von Gerkan, Professor von Busse & Partners, and Kaup, Scholz, Wortmann.

The Busse team won in 1976 but work was interrupted for four years in 1981 by a court battle. When work resumed, changes were necessary, including widening the building by 10 metres, extending the passenger facilities from three to four modules and incorporating an arrivals gallery to segregate arriving and departing passengers.

Competitive procedures were also followed to establish the fit-out of the terminal. Lighting designers were invited to submit ideas for the 900-metre gallery which links station, car parks and car rental. Keith Sonnier of New York was awarded the contract.

The competition for the Technical Region North, a 1,200 by 200 metre strip, was won by architects Schmidt-Schicketanz & Partners of Munich and that for the cargo handling facilities by Zobel, Weber, Weissenfeldt, also of Munich. The giant hangars for jumbo jets were subject to very stringent requirements laid down by the airlines. The solution was to produce official designs prepared by architects Günter Büschl, of Munich, working with Professor Fred Angerer. These were made available to construction companies for competitive bids.

At surface level (Level 04), the terminal appears as a complex of six major buildings laid out according to the twin principles of symmetry and axiality. The terminal itself, seen to best effect on the apron approach, is an imposing, long building punctuated by twenty evenly spaced airbridges. On the landside it is formed into four projecting pavilions containing departure halls A, B, C and D. Between, and set back from the roadway to provide space for waiting vehicles, are the arrival halls. The pick-up points are covered by overall canopies (surprisingly rare at airports) which provide shelter from rain and sun, for passengers loading or unloading baggage into or out of cars.

Groups of check-in desks, leading through to departure lounges, alternate with baggage claim areas; thus, for those familiar with the airport, walks to and from the planes can be quite short, particularly when being dropped off or met by car or taxi, rather than taking the S-Bahn. By contrast, visitors unsure of their check-in point, or needing to use a series of facilities, can find themselves walking a very long way indeed, effectively the length of four whole terminals.

To those arriving by road, the orderliness of the landscaping is calming and impressive. While many airports consist of unremitting acres of tarmac, at Munich there are extensive, trim lawns, and lines of well tended trees, pleasing to the eye and creating a tranquil effect. Opposite, ranged in perfect symmetry, are four (five-storey) parking garages, largely disguised by luxuriantly planted sloping earth banks.

In the centre, in a position which in previous centuries might have been occupied by a great chapel or banqueting hall, is a pivotal building containing shops and restaurants. For passengers arriving by train, this building connects via a broad concourse to the main terminal building. Passengers proceed to check-in at arrival points at this level using a 900-metre corridor equipped with moving walkways, and ascend via escalators and lifts to one of the four departure halls. This space is illuminated and enlivened along its whole length by Keith Sonnier's dramatic, glowing light sculpture.

For the terminal, Professor von Busse and his colleagues set their sights beyond mere function:

Airports can enhance our range of experience. Imagination must take precedence if sheer size and technology are to be bearable and if flying is to be an adventure.

The key to the design was light – diffuse, indirect and direct:

Light needs solid form to create effect. Form and colour enhance it, on surfaces, on edges and profiles, and through shadows. Unsurpassed in this respect is the colour white, the most demanding and expressive of all colours.

They emphasised light's ability to impart a feeling of openness, expanse and trust – all intrinsically pleasant qualities.

Their choice of white was based partly on Bavarian Baroque architecture where interiors, whether in churches or great staircase halls, are a brilliant, often all-over white. Bright colours have therefore not been used in the airport, silver being used for technical elements, in the form of zinc, aluminium and stainless steel. The only exceptions are the flight information boards which have white lettering on a lavender blue ground.

White is also predominate in the spacious and lofty seating areas at the departure gates, where it is used for columns, exposed steelwork and window framing. The same white livery appears on the apron outside, the roofing and window trim and the white control tower looming behind.

The other striking quality of the interior is transparency. The airside is divided into departure lounges, with separate corridors for arrivals, departures and connecting flights, but almost everywhere the partitions are of glass opening up views to the outside world, and, at certain points, allowing those on the landside a rare and welcome glimpse of the world beyond passport control and customs.

The arrivals halls are not low-ceilinged and windowless, as is typical in many airports, but are double-height and top-lit. Instead of the frequent feeling of being closeted, people are visible at different levels, using glass-sided overhead walkways. Even the airbridges and associated staircase towers are glass walled (with white trim, of course) offering the visual excitement of early modern classics with their transparent staircase towers.

Impressive efforts have been made to make restaurants, cafes and snack bars as stylish as the smartest in town. In the restaurants, 'international cliché and provincial plainness have no place,' the architects remark. The decor of the two restaurants makes use of white, black, silver and ultramarine. From Trattoria Monaco and Il Mondo there are extensive views through glass walls and roofs and fantastic lights designed by Ingo Maurer. The snack bars are equally distinctive and slick, designed by Professor Franz-Xavier Lutz and partner, Suzanne Wiegner, and assisted by the

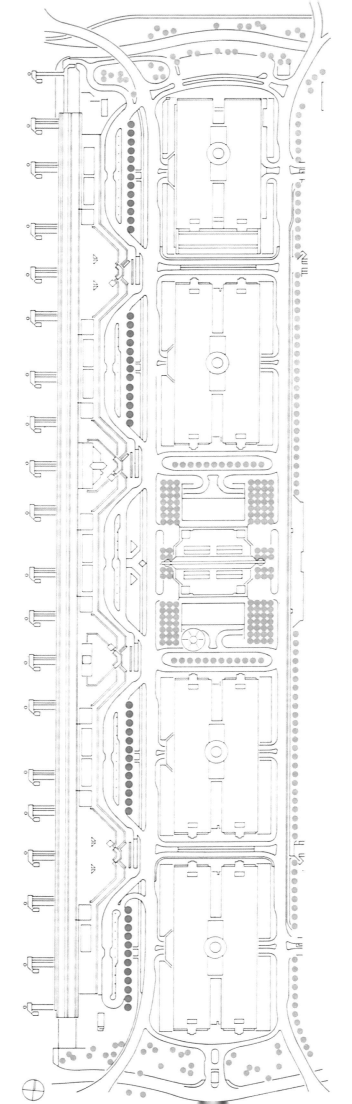

painters Hans Baschang and Rupprecht Geiger, the sculptor Eduardo Paolozzi and the video artist Marie-Jo Lafontaine.

In all respects, this is one of the most impressively harmonious and relaxing of all recent airports. The big question is whether, as it grows, jarring new elements will creep in. A sudden call by Lufthansa for a special flight operations centre at a very late stage caused serious headaches. However, the Munich Airport Authority is determined to overcome any such pressures. Moreover, it upholds a strong belief in the functional and aesthetic significance of buildings, which it asserts should retain their attractiveness for all users.

A major new commercial centre is under construction. This is located centrally and set across the approach road from the main terminal. With a soaring arched roof, this centre will become the dominating landmark of the whole airport. Begun in March 1996, it is scheduled for completion in 1999. Planned around a large covered area, it will offer 31,000 square metres of office space. In addition, a new Terminal 2 is due to open in 2003 which will serve Lufthansa and its associated airlines.

General plan of landscaping, approach roads and parking

ABOVE AND CENTRE: Computer-generated views of exterior and interior; BELOW AND OPPOSITE: Model views

JOHN F KENNEDY AIRPORT, TERMINAL 1
New York, US

This elegant design pays homage to Eero Saarinen's famous TWA terminal at JFK (1956–62), notably in the swooping silhouette on the approach side. While Saarinen's building was remarkable for its powerful sculptural handling of concrete, Bodouva's design is altogether lighter and more transparent, making appropriate use of more advanced materials and technology. Yet, like its precursor, it still dips down over the entrance with the roofs rising up on either side suggestive of wings and flight.

The new Terminal 1 is a $450 million facility designed for a consortium of four international carriers – Air France, Korean Air, JAL and Lufthansa – and it is the first new terminal at JFK for twenty-five years. William Nicholas Bodouva was selected after a national competition and the terminal was designed and built using a 'fast-track' process. It stands on a 14.5 hectare site, encompassing an area of 60,400 square metres, at the entrance to JFK from the Van Wyck Expressway.

With floor-to-roof glass running round the upper departure level and extensive roof glazing this is a modern day glass palace. Abundant daylight floods down to the lower arrivals level and even into the 'sterile corridors' preceding passport control. The steel structure allows wide spans over the departure hall, using steel girders and tension rods. The roof is single ply.

The 230-metre-long departure hall houses four banks of island counters with ninety-eight check-in desks. Passengers pass through a single security point to the airside departure area with a mezzanine above housing the airline lounges. Both levels have spectacular views over the apron to the Manhattan skyline.

Behind the crescent-shaped terminal are eleven gates (and two hardstands for 747-400 aircraft), the majority approached along a broad finger pier.

The building was required to meet New York State energy codes. In order to reduce overheating or solar gain, glass exposed to sunlight is fritted. Sheldon D Wander, Senior Vice President at WNB+A explains, 'Solid strips of Teflon are baked on the glass creating the effect of Venetian blinds.' The glass has a greyish tint to further reduce heat penetration.

The building's appearance is spectacular at night when internal lighting (all reflected) reveals its openness and transparency to the full, as well as the slenderness of the constructional elements – whether wafer-thin roof or glass walls set in slender mullions. The ground level 'meeters and greeters' hall also has extensive glazing. In addition, light floods down through open balconies.

Construction was started in 1995 and the new terminal was opened and became operational on 28 May 1998.

Model views and watercolour of exterior

OSLO GARDERMOEN AIRPORT
Norway

Oslo's new airport is the biggest land development project ever undertaken in Norway. Begun in August 1993, it was opened on 8 October 1998, and will cater for an estimated twelve million passengers a year. Air traffic to Oslo's existing Fornebu Airport had more than tripled over twenty years and it was operating at full capacity. An Act of Parliament in 1992 designated Gardermoen, an existing military airbase, as the country's main airport for the future. The estimated cost was 11.4 billion Norwegian Kroner (NOK).

From the air, the new airport resembles a large 'H' with two parallel runways that can operate independently, providing a combined capacity of seventy-four aircraft movements per hour. The existing 3,300-metre runway has been extended by 300 metres, and a new runway of 2,950 metres built 2 kilometres to the east. The main terminal will be located midway between them. Measuring 165 by 115 metres, with an 819-metre-long pier serving departure gates, it is planned on two main levels – arrivals, as usual on the ground floor, with departures above. There are thirty-four departure gates, with up to sixteen remote stands. Norway's second largest railway station serves the terminal, with four through lines and three 350-metre-long platforms. For maximum convenience this is centrally sited on the lower ground floor level of the terminal.

It is intended that the airport will be served by six high-speed trains every hour running in both directions to central Oslo, with a journey time of nineteen minutes. The 48-kilometre double-track railway is designed for operational speeds of 200 kilometres per hour, with a check-in facility at Oslo Central Station. Local and intercity trains will also serve the airport, and a multi-storey car park with some 4,000 spaces will be built to the south of the main terminal.

The terminal is planned on the model of Kansai International Airport, comprising a wave-roofed main building and a long departure concourse, Pier A, extending left and right, with airbridges on both sides towards the ends. A parallel twelve-gate Pier B, reached by a tunnel under the taxiway, will be added later.

The terminal is intended to be a showcase of Norwegian building traditions, using natural materials, notably wooden roofs and stone floors. The competition-winning design had shown a tubular steel roof but the Norwegian Government subsequently insisted – sixteen months after the design had begun – that the terminal should be built with home-grown timber. As the layout of the terminal had been fixed by this stage, the timber roof required very large structural spans.

Chris Wise and Alistair Lenczner of engineers Ove Arup & Partners, helped devise a system of paired lattice beams set 3 metres apart. The overall 136-metre length of each beam is claimed to be the longest in the world. The primary beams are carried on concrete trees, each with four steel branches which stretch out diagonally to support the beams and bring the spans down to 45 metres. The secondary beams are of glue laminated soft wood. The result is one of the largest timber roofs ever built. Timber also has a good fire-rating and is 'self-finishing'.

Natural materials provide most of the colour in the building. The wood is principally oak and maple. Much of the stone is imported marble as, surprisingly, though Norway is a country of mountains, it was not possible to obtain local stone in sufficient quantities. Architect Niels Torp comments:

> From the start I wanted the layout to be very simple so you would never be in doubt of your way to the airside or the landside. In my view

many airports are very confusing in this respect.
I wanted it to be almost a building without signs
with the maximum sense of openness.

Torps also wanted openness to pervade arrivals and departures. He explains:

Very often arrivals and departures seem to be
totally different buildings. Our concept was one
room, two levels, but we have had to seal off
floors because of security requirements.

However, the simplicity is maintained, and departing passengers continue all the way to the gate on one level while disembarking passengers descend to arrivals level as they leave the airbridge.

The departure hall is planned with sixty-four check-in desks grouped on three islands and an 820-metre-long, thirty-four gate concourse. In front of the terminal a new 90-metre-high control tower provides a conspicuous landmark for everyone arriving by road. It is called the *Baune*, after an old Danish word for look-out tower.

The airport is 47 kilometres from the centre of Oslo and occupies an area of 13 square kilometres, on which houses, farms and business premises have been purchased to clear the way for development. The new airport is intended to route flight paths away from densely populated areas, reducing the number of local people affected by noise from 60,000 at Fornebu to just 3,000. The authorities insist that a strong emphasis will be placed on the preservation of landscape and vegetation.

Total public investment in the project is estimated at NOK 20 billion, including NOK 11.4 billion for the airport (covering compensation to the armed forces), and NOK 4.6 billion for the railway. The new airport is expected to handle about 11 million passengers in its first year rising to 15 million a year when it operates at peak capacity.

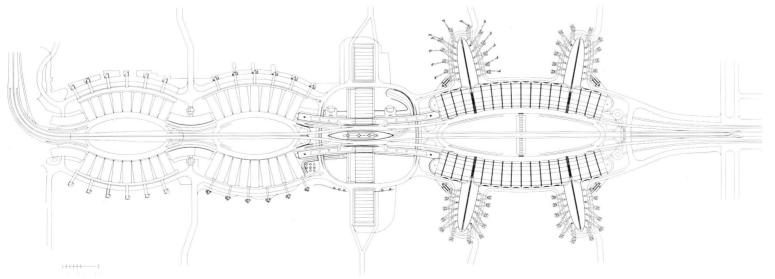

AÉROPORTS DE PARIS
CHARLES DE GAULLE AIRPORT, TERMINAL 2F
Paris, France

Charles de Gaulle International Airport is the masterwork of the greatest and most prolific airport designer of our age, Paul Andreu, chief architect of Aéroports de Paris. Andreu began with the remarkable circular Terminal 1 and then shifted the focus of the airport to Terminal 2, developing a new series of terminals along a grand axis – the layout that has become his hallmark around the world. Here is the scale and formality of the grand manner, combined with a Los Angeles style love of swooping curving roadways.

Terminals 2A, 2B, 2C and 2D are laid out on either side of two oval road rings, a fact that is soon embedded in the mind of anyone taking the airport transfer bus from one terminal to another. These crescent or banana shaped terminals were planned on the sprint principle – a businessperson in a hurry, dropped outside the right airline desk, would have no more than 50 metres between car and plane. The system works well when the aircraft is on time, but if there are delays, passengers can be corralled in holdrooms away from shops and bars, wondering whether to battle their way back out through the security system.

Terminal 2F (the first finger pier opened in 1998) is intended to be balanced by a matching Terminal 2E. It is therefore more spacious than its predecessors, with two finger piers where passengers can enjoy greater space and mobility as well as a wider selection of shops. The new module has precisely double the capacity of its predecessors. While Terminals 2A-D have powerfully sculpted concrete roofs, creating a cavernous effect, the 140-metre-long finger piers, or peninsulas, of 2F have curving glass walls and a form of steel space-frame roof. This creates memorably calm and radiant spaces. The departures area is above, as usual, with arrivals situated below, achieving complete separation.

This is extended even to the airbridges, formed in a continuous descending hairpin loop with the telescopic arm to the aircraft door set on the curve. In accordance with the latest trend, these are also glass sided. In all, there are twenty-two aircraft stands served by airbridges, with twenty-one remote stands. Functional levels are arranged internally as follows: Level 0: runway, baggage handling and passenger arrival. Level 1: passenger disembarkation. Level 2: passenger departure.

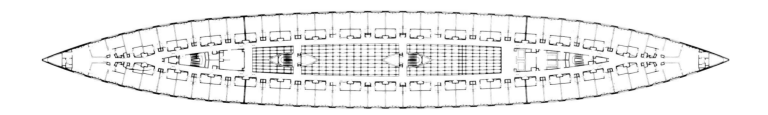

OPPOSITE, FROM ABOVE: Computer-generated perspective of interior; masterplan; ABOVE: Standard floor plan, exchange module

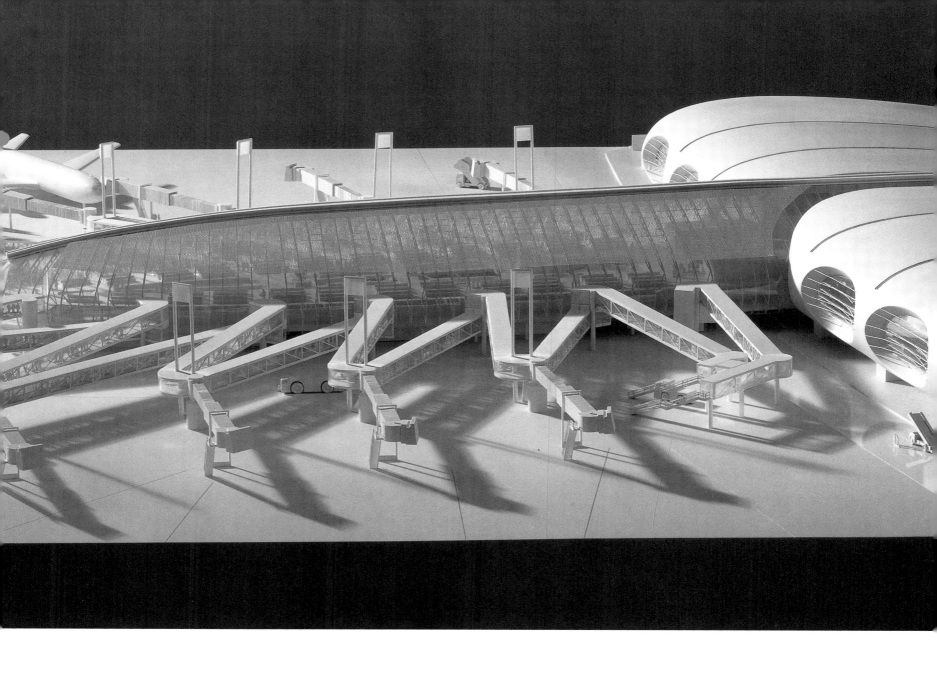

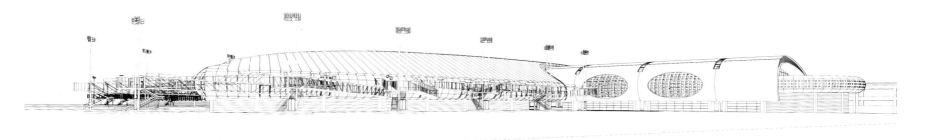

FROM ABOVE: Model exterior; elevation

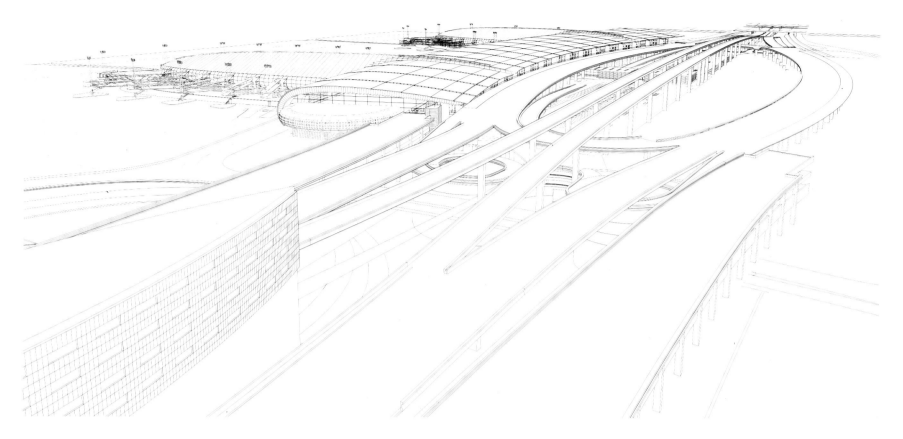

Exterior geometry

The central section between the roadway contains a 3,300-space, three-level underground car park. To enhance the drama of the design, the central reservation will be crossed by two swooping roadways bypassing the new terminal, sailing over the ringway at either end. The concrete roofs of the departure hall are once again shaped expressively and sculpturally, emphasised by a continuous curve. On the airside, overlooking the aprons, there are huge oval windows which, from outside, resemble headlights set in a sports car bonnet.

Between Terminals 2A-D and the new Terminal 2F, is a spectacular new railway station designed by Andreu with the great Irish engineer Peter Rice. In accordance with the exact geometry that marks the whole layout, the railway bisects the axis of the roadways at precisely ninety degrees. Here, Andreu displays the same mastery of inter-locking levels and functions as in his original Terminal 1 – the difference being that there the

geometry was circular and here it is rectangular. The exceptions lie with the hotel set above the centre of the station, which is a distinctive torpedo shape, and the gentle curves of the roadways.

The station (which is illustrated and described in *The Architecture of Rail*, published by Academy Editions), comprises two symmetrical halves. The cross section shows the eight tracks and three island platforms; two of the tracks are for non-stop TGVs passing through the station. The lines serve a new RER rapid link to Paris as well as TGVs skirting Paris and connecting with Lille, London and Brussels to the north, and Lyons and other destinations to the south. The multi-level station also houses a bubble-car rail system (ST) linking Terminal 1 with terminals 2A-D. Upper levels contain a business centre, shops and restaurants.

The estimated construction cost of Terminal 2F at 1992 values was 2.5 billion FF. The estimated construction cost of the station (opened in November 1994) was 1,150 million FF at 1991 values.

ABOVE: Computer-generated perspective of interior

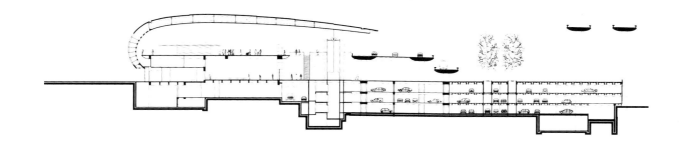

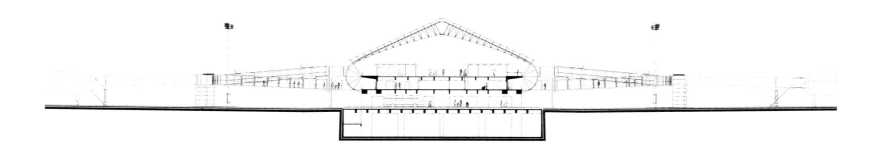

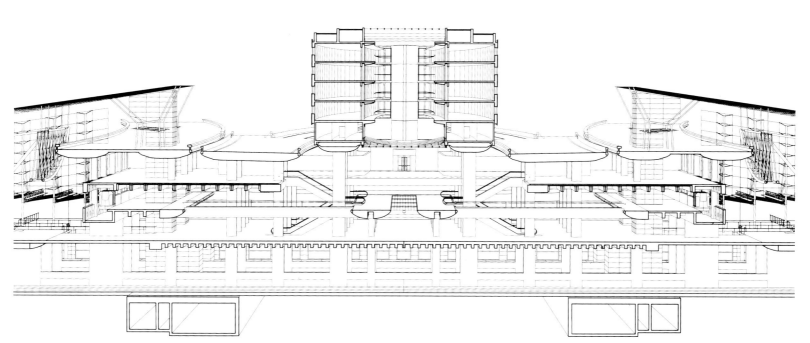

FROM ABOVE: Sections; perspective cross section of hotel and TGV station, the exchange module

TASSO KATSELAS ASSOCIATES
PITTSBURGH AIRPORT, NEW TERMINAL
Pennsylvania, US

Pittsburgh handled 20 million passengers in 1995; 32 million are forecast for 2003, with aircraft movements predicted to rise from 425,000 to 544,000 in the same period. The airport authority states that there are 71 million potential passengers living within a 725-kilometre radius, representing one hour's flying time.

The layout of the airport pioneered the concept of the 'straight-ahead' design: three key buildings are here linked by automated walkways, with parking (17,420 spaces) at one end and aircraft at the other. No parking space is more than 245 metres from a walkway. The walkways are glass-enclosed, heated and air-conditioned, and begin in the open-air parking lot (with extended term, then long-term parking), continuing through the short-term parking garage (where car rental is sited) into the landside terminal that provides check-in, baggage handling and airport offices.

Passengers progress through security into the twenty-five gate commuter terminal which has three short piers (laid out on an E-plan) ensuring minimum walking times. Alternatively, they may continue straight on, via an underground people mover running beneath the aprons and taxiways to the airside terminal – the one-kilometre journey takes sixty seconds. This is an island building on an X-plan, a design minimising walking distances to the seventy-five gates and equipped with moving walkways along each arm.

The airport claims that this layout reduces taxiing distances for aircraft, permitting shorter turnaround times. Twelve automated de-icing towers located near the ends of runways enable planes to be de-iced immediately before take-off.

The central core of the X-plan airside terminal contains 9,290 square metres of retail space. This was introduced (and is managed by) BAA

Pittsburgh Inc, a subsidiary of BAA plc, the British Airports Authority which owns and operates seven airports in the United Kingdom. Pittsburgh Airport is a connecting hub, and the airmall – the airport's invention – is designed for passengers with a spare hour or two in which to eat and shop. The airmall introduced 'street pricing', breaking with the practice of giving sole rights to a single concessionaire which could charge as it liked. Retail tenants are obliged to keep prices as low as in their outlets elsewhere.

Pittsburgh is renowned as the home of the American steel industry. The airport is constructed of materials manufactured locally: steel, aluminium, glass and concrete. The arched steel truss roof of the landside terminal is a conscious echo of the steel and glass roofs of great turn-of-the-century railway termini, while the barrel vaults of the concourse arms are in modern precast concrete. The buff, grey, red, blue and silver colour scheme has been chosen by the architects as 'symbolic of life, journeying from earth to sky by technology'.

George Perinis, the project architect, recalls the construction history:

> The competition was held as long ago as 1979, and the project went through a series of refinements. We broke ground on 26 June 1987 and it took two years to move 20,000 cubic yards of soil. But we were 100 per cent ready at the opening, with the garages, parking and the automated baggage system up and running and all the shops present.

Actual construction of the project, which cost $800 million, commenced on 1 July 1989, and it opened on 1 October 1992. It also included the building of a new runway, aprons and taxiways, a 32 million litres fuel farm, aircraft hangars and a control tower.

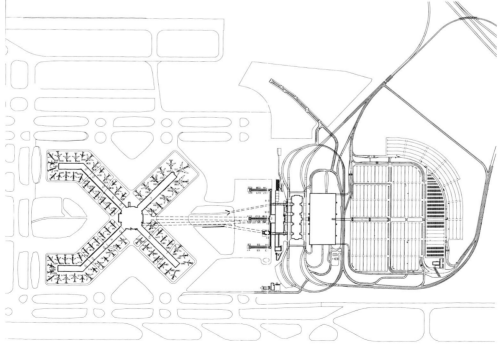

Plan

POINTE À PITRE INTERNATIONAL AIRPORT
Guadaloupe

This new terminal is built on a virgin site on the other side of the runway from its predecessor, and intended, in the words of the architects, 'to show the varied Caribbean landscape in a nutshell'.

It has been built with a ground-level arrivals hall and an upstairs departure hall reached by an elevated road. The plan is compact and laid out with the perfect symmetry that is a hallmark of Paul Andreu, the chief architect of Aéroports de Paris. Architects take pleasure in a building's section and here, like the plan, it is satisfyingly symmetrical, with matching gently curved roofs suggestive of flight. There is also a neat visual correspondence between the airbridges on the apron and the 'land' bridges linking the elevated road to the departures hall.

The section also shows the easy flow from landside to airside at departures level, with escalators and stairs connecting, scissors fashion, to the arrivals hall below. Ease of movement to and from planes is maximised by the up and down ramps on the airbridges, which avoid the situation where arriving passengers have to walk up to departures level before descending to the arrivals hall. The architects also make ingenious use of double-height spaces to increase the sense of openness and airiness by combining the mezzanine level with the upper or lower hall at different points. Thus the baggage reclaim hall is double height, and on both land and airsides the mezzanine is open to the departure hall above, allowing light to flood down from the tall, almost 20-metre-high glass walls.

Front and back facades incline inward to reduce solar gain, while the vertical windows on the flanks are perforated metal screens filtering the amount of sun entering the terminal. A similar effect is achieved, front and back, with the use of perforated metal fins which break-up steep directional sunlight but allow extensive views out.

The sense of coolness, in contrast to the heat outside, is heightened by the pale palette of colours. Slatted screens (like the characteristic West Indian jalousies) are used on the pillars containing the airhandling plant; underfoot, the highly reflective floors look as cool as sheets of water.

In 1996, the year it opened, the terminal won the award for the best metal construction organised by the French Metal Construction Consortium.

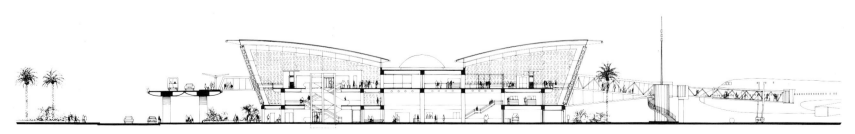

Section

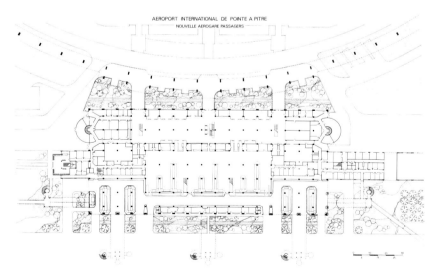

AEROPORT INTERNATIONAL DE POINTE A PITRE
NOUVELLE AEROGARE PASSAGERS

Plan of arrivals level

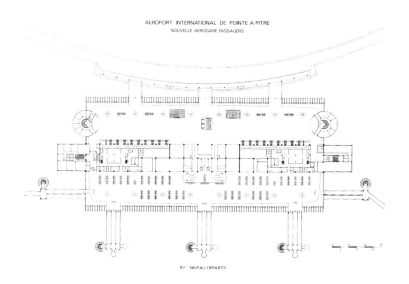

AEROPORT INTERNATIONAL DE POINTE A PITRE
NOUVELLE AEROGARE PASSAGERS

R2 NIVEAU DEPARTS

Plan of departures level

Computer-generated perspectives of exterior

SAN FRANCISCO AIRPORT, NEW TERMINAL

California, US

The central feature of this exhilarating design is a huge wing-like roof, its gently arched forms more suggestive of a bird in flight than a plane. It oversails the glass walls on every side. The essence of the design is the use of two sets of enormous cantilever trusses, reminiscent of those used for the mighty Forth Bridge, constructed in Scotland just over a century ago. In a similar manner, the great steel trusses extend to support a central section that floats above the ground without support from below.

In addition, the building is a tribute to one of SOM's own pioneering designs: the jet maintenance hangar, built in 1958 for United Airlines and demolished in 1996. New aircraft such as the Boeing 707 and the Douglas DC-8 required larger maintenance facilities. In response, the architects created a cantilever structure spanning out 45 metres on either side from the central supports, creating a space that was wide enough to house four of United's new DC-8s. SOM's principal designer, Myron Goldsmith, said in a 1990 interview that he had wanted to sheathe the hangar in glass to reveal the spectacular structure within, but for reasons of cost this was prevented.

The new terminal realises Goldsmith's dream. It is the centrepiece of the airport's current expansion programme and includes all facilities for international arrivals and departures, with duty-free shops, restaurants and airline lounges. It is also the central point on the airport's new light rail system. Departure gates are set along finger piers extending diagonally from the terminal.

The design is more dramatic as the point at which the roof dips down is the very centre of a huge concourse. Standing inside, the roof has no support from below just at the point at which it seems to be vital. A glass curtain-wall along the front is too insubstantial to take the weight, and the clusters of four pencil columns look quite inadequate to the task. Yet the roof, like the walls, is lightness itself; slender steel trusses which in further defiance of gravity support not the solid parts of the roof but the glass slits between.

This is a terminal which will glow sensationally at night when the uplit roof structure will reveal the filigree slenderness of much of the steel-work used for the glass curtain-wall and roof. The floorspace within the terminal is 150,000 square metres.

SOM, working with Del Campo & Maru, and Michael Willis & Associates, was the winner of the competition sponsored by the airport. Only invited participants were eligible. The design process was begun in 1994 and completion is scheduled for 2000.

Site plan

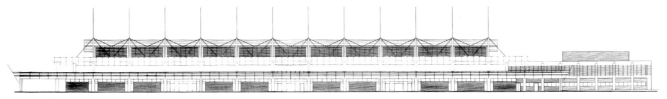

North elevation

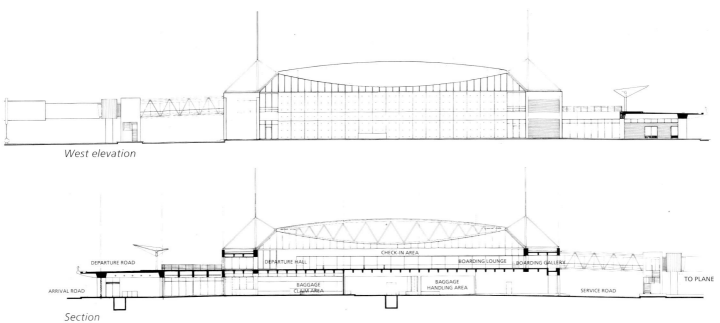

West elevation

Section

DEPARTURE ROAD DEPARTURE HALL CHECK-IN AREA BOARDING LOUNGE BOARDING GALLERY

ARRIVAL ROAD BAGGAGE CLAIM AREA BAGGAGE HANDLING AREA SERVICE ROAD TO PLANE

SANYA PHOENIX AIRPORT, NEW TERMINAL

China

This stylish but modest-sized new terminal was designed to handle a million passengers a year. Costing an estimated 180 million FF, the terminal became operational in July 1994. It consists of two main levels, incorporating an upper departures hall, served by an elevated three-lane road set on the roof of the arrivals hall which is situated below. In a break with traditional airport design, the canopy is not attached to the departures hall but is freestanding, as on an island platform in a railway station.

The white cladding of the roof gives the terminal a sleek modern look, and a festive touch is added by the twenty-four prominent white flagpoles set in two rows along the roof. Each of these is held in place by diagonal steel braces which enliven the silhouette of the building by suggesting a row of pyramid roofs. A futuristic element is contributed by the lozenge-shaped roof trusses, which at the ends of the terminal resemble a slice through a flying saucer. The use of these wide zig-zag trusses allows the creation of a broad column-free hall containing the check-in areas and boarding lounges and boarding gallery or concourse.

Domestic departures are located on one side, with international departures on the other, a pattern which is repeated on the arrivals level below where there are sixteen check-in counters and two luggage carousels. The two airbridges span an airside service road connecting to telescopic gangways. Six planes can be accommodated alongside the terminal. In addition, four remote parking stands are served by bus.

Four hundred carparking spaces are provided at ground level in front of the arrival hall.

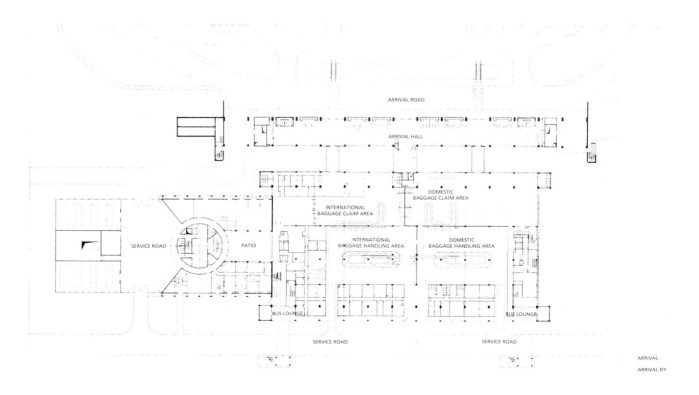

Ground-floor plan

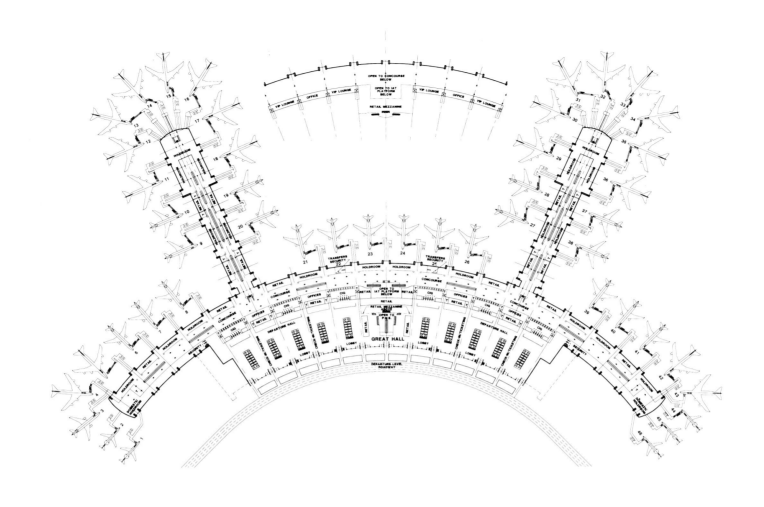

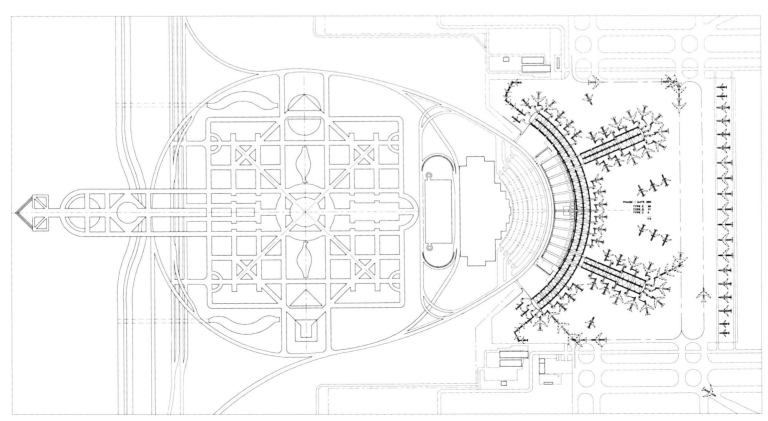

FROM ABOVE: Plan of VIP lounges and departures area; plan of aircraft parking

C W FENTRESS, J H BRADBURN AND ASSOCIATES WITH BHJW
INCHON INTERNATIONAL AIRPORT
Seoul, Korea

The new Inchon Airport, like Kansai, is to be situated on a specially created artificial island. Known as Yong Jong Do Island, it will lie in the Yellow Sea, 16 kilometres offshore from the city of Inchon and some 48 kilometres west of Seoul city centre. On completion in 2002, all of the capital's long-haul air traffic will be transferred to the new airport.

The competition, launched in 1992, for the $550 million new main terminal building at Inchon was won by Fentress Bradburn which put forward its schematic design in the following year. The design proceeded to the development phase in 1997 and opening is currently set for January 2001.

The new terminal is radial or crescent-shaped with two piers projecting at right angles providing forty-six gates around a compact perimeter so that walking distances are nowhere more than 365 metres. The masterplan provides for up to four parallel island concourses (Atlanta-style) bringing the total number of gates to 174, with the capacity to accommodate up to 100 million passengers a year.

The design, like that of Doha, is intended to incorporate resonances from local tradition. As Curt Fentress explains:

> The swooping rooflines are a modern interpretation of historic Korean architecture. Symbolically, the form reflects both the aerodynamic shapes of planes, as well as the rolling waves on the shore. The masts supporting the roof are an echo of the ships in Inchon Harbour.

Fentress adds that the form of the terminal 'represents the juxtaposition of earth and sky'. As

he explains, the lower levels are mainly solid, using concrete and more massive materials, while the upper departure levels become lighter with the use of glass and steel symbolising sky and flight.

The overall design envisages a Versailles-style, grand axial layout with elaborate patterns of parallel and intersecting roads and taxiways and four north–south runways. The approach roads form a giant egg-shaped loop, inset with a perfect symmetrical grid of roads that, on plan, resembles an elaborate geometric garden design.

Gardens are certainly incorporated as well as lakes and basins of water. Beyond, the axis is prolonged as a giant pier or rather a solid artificial peninsula projecting into the sea like a compass point. The plan shows the four phases leading to 'ultimate build-out', starting with only one runway.

The essence of the design lies in the bold and varied roofs, beginning with the dramatically arched canopy over the curving drop-off road. Inside, the check-in hall will impress not by loftiness but by cavernous proportions with the ultimate in gravity defying broad 'depressed' arches spanning from side to side. They are supported by bowstring trusses braced laterally by ties anchored to a series of suspended posts, their tapering form suggestive of stalactites.

The roofs over the departure concourses are arched inversely, rising towards the edges and supported from masts, to create a swept-up profile suggestive of temple architecture. Seen in profile, approaching by road, the combination of gentle convex and concave forms will possess tremendous grace.

Model and artist's rendering of new airport

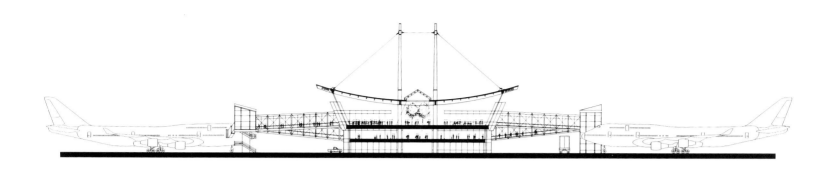

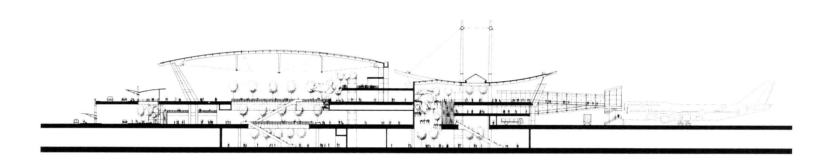

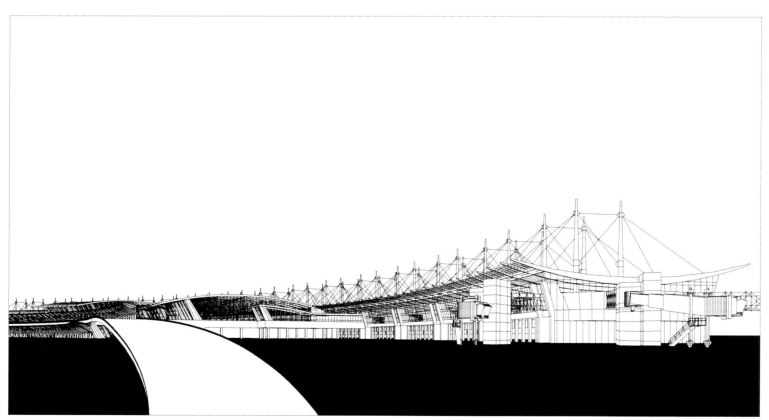

FROM ABOVE: Sections; perspective

ABOVE: Artist's renderings of interior; BELOW: Elevation

ABOVE: Artist's renderings of interior; BELOW: Elevation

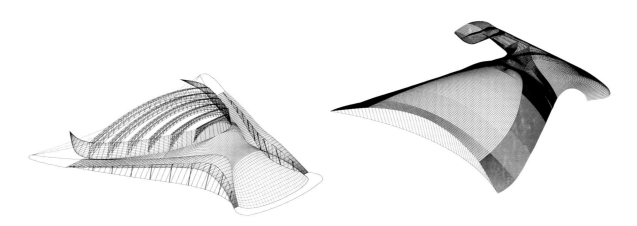

FROM ABOVE: Roof geometry; computer-generated perspective

TERRY FARRELL & PARTNERS, WITH SAMOO AND DMJM
INCHON TRANSPORTATION CENTRE
Seoul, Korea

This facility, for the Korean Airport Construction Authority, is conceived as the grand gateway to Inchon International Airport. Connecting to Fentress Bradburn's new terminal, it will form the point of entry for all means of transport – train, car, limousine, taxi or coach. Below ground, the Transportation Centre houses the platforms for four railway lines, while at ground level the approach road curves to provide a generous length of parking for both drop-off and pick-up. In addition, there are four levels of below-surface parking with the capacity to accommodate up to 5,000 vehicles.

Passengers may progress to the terminal (and back) on no less than three levels, moving up to departures or down to arrivals as necessary. If they miss the first escalator or elevator they can take a subsequent one. Alternatively, they can ascend to the topmost level and take the automatic people mover train straight through to Terminal 1.

Externally, the building began life on the drawing board as a metaphor for flight, with a tower suggestive of the head and neck of a crane – a bird which in Korea is invested with a rich symbolism. However, the financial crisis in Asia has imposed certain modifications. The proposed high-speed rail link will no longer be built but a fast train link will take passengers to and from Seoul in thirty-five to forty minutes. The tower, which was originally intended to house the controllers directing planes on the aprons and taxiways, is no longer necessary as these facilities are to be provided elsewhere.

Therefore, the architects had to provide a new focal climax to the monumental building. This is achieved by constructing a giant oculus in the roof, surmounting it with a massive glass aerofoil they call the Jewel. This 35 by 15 metre feature has a suction effect, accelerating the rise of air out of the top of the building. Internally the Transportation Centre will take the form of a Great Hall with spectacular 180-metre spans. The roof is supported on huge steel lattice V-beams formed of tubular elements and inset with large areas of fritted glass.

There are three main levels below ground. The lowest of these contains tunnels for an automatic train which is intended to take passengers non-stop to Terminal 1 and to the future Terminal 2. Above this are the four tracks of the Seoul rail link. On the third level – which is still below ground level – is the main floor of the Great Hall, which connects through to the arrivals level in Terminal 1.

The competition to design the Transportation Centre was won by the Farrell Partnership in 1996 and construction commenced in 1997. The facility is scheduled for completion in 2002. A stipulation of the client is that all specialist subcontracts have to be met in Korea; a very different scenario from construction arrangements at Chek Lap Kok, where materials were imported from many different parts of the world.

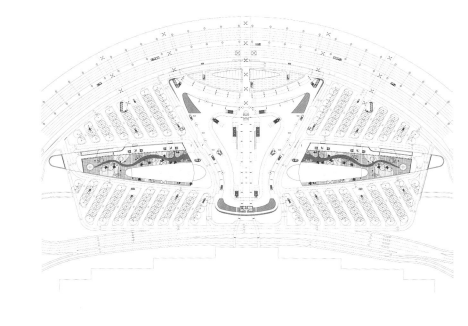

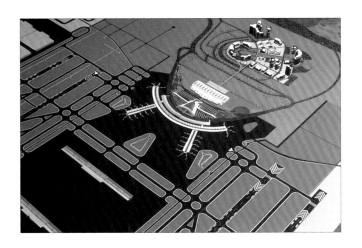

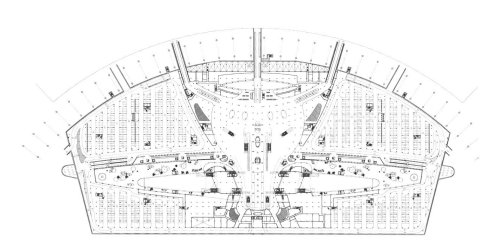

LEFT: Computer drawings of terminal and site; RIGHT: Plans

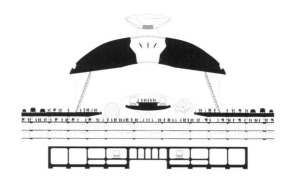

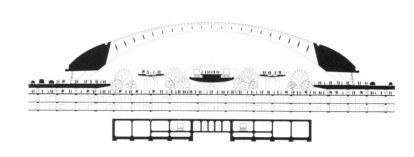

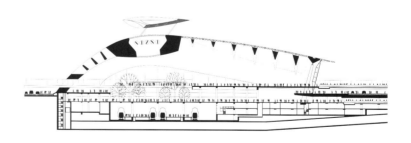

LEFT: Model views; RIGHT: Sections

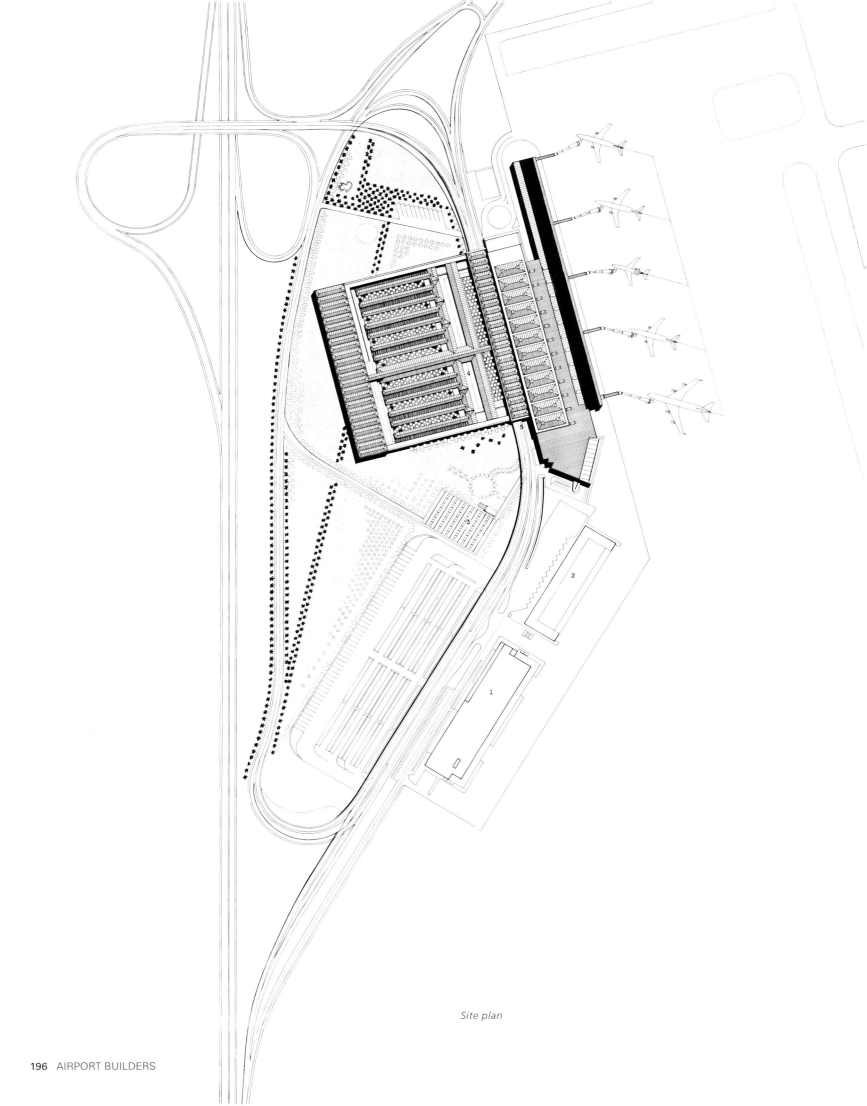

Site plan

JOSEF RAFAEL MONEO
SAN PABLO AIRPORT
Seville, Spain

Rafael Moneo's new airport is *sui generis*, unlike any other. It resembles a military fortress, so massive and windowless are the walls. In beautiful contrast, the silhouette of repeating roofs is like that of an eighteenth- or nineteenth-century malt-house.

The airport was built for the 1992 Seville World Expo. Moneo explains how he set out to break with established tradition:

> The architectural design of airports has from its inception insistently sought to approximate the sophisticated industrial world of aeronautics through its imagery while inevitably using the techniques and methods of the construction industry . . . Experience has taught us that an airport cannot be compared to an airplane, whether in terms of materials or in terms of form. The perfection and lightness of flying machines have little in common with the complex functional mechanisms that are airports. Airports belong to the world of things built on land, and not to the sky, and are by definition places of transit.

Moneo compares his airport with projects by Le Corbusier where the highway penetrates the building. He explains that the road to the city centre determines the geometry of parallel linear walls. The parking area on one side is a key element of the complex, conceived as a patio where shaded parking bays alternate with rows of orange trees. From here, covered walkways lead to arrivals downstairs and departures above.

The departure hall is the greatest surprise of all: a modern Alhambra among airports, with a series of beehive vaults that have the massiveness usually associated with medieval structures. These are ranged in two parallel lines and supported on huge arches that recall the work of Louis Sullivan in Chicago. What makes them distinctly Andalucian is the almost Moorish perspectives of arches seen both diagonally and in perfect enfilade. We are accustomed to columns with capitals or entablatures jutting out a fraction from the arches above; here, the circular columns are significantly more slender than the imposts of the arches and the transition is made by a distinctive inward-sloping capital almost like a jelly mould.

Most striking is the astonishing sense of cool and calm generated by the deep blue of the beehive vaults. In the hot Andalucian summer the small oculi at the top admit sufficient daylight to illuminate the interior while ensuring that the concourse feels cool and shaded.

This may seem a large building for what is a relatively small airport. Its one drawback is that beyond passport control there is no real airside concourse with shops or cafes and the passenger can be stranded in the gate departure lounge with nowhere to obtain refreshments or a newspaper.

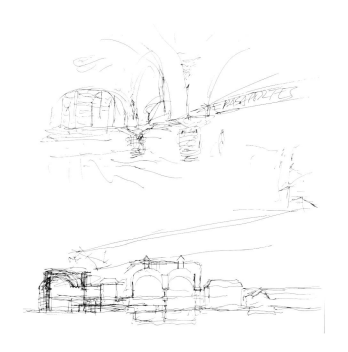

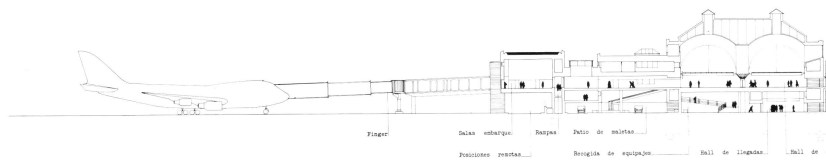

Finger   Salas embarque   Rampas   Patio de maletas

Posiciones remotas   Recogida de equipajes   Hall de llegadas   Hall de s

Section

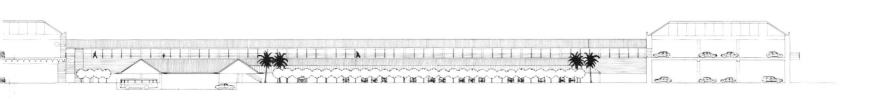

FROM ABOVE: Bird's-eye rendering of future development; plans of phase 1 and final phase

AÉROPORTS DE PARIS
SHANGHAI PUDONG AIRPORT, NEW TERMINAL
Shanghai, China

This major terminal, currently under construction for one of the world's fastest growing cities, has been designed by the architects, engineers and planners of Aéroports de Paris (ADP). Like Terminals 2A–D at Charles de Gaulle, it is planned along a central grand axis, running north–south, with the runways set parallel on either side. Future growth, on a spectacular scale, is allowed for with provision for a second phase which will largely repeat the module of the first.

The layout is simplicity itself. In the first phase, there are two matching terminals for domestic and international traffic. Each terminal has two main levels, with departures situated above and arrivals below. The departure and arrival concourses are set centrally, leading through to a long transverse pier which extends at both ends so aircraft can park on either side. The gently rising arched roofs are intended, according to Aéoports de Paris, to evoke the wings of a bird and to symbolise the flight of the city of Shanghai towards the twenty-first century.

The architects have sought to achieve maximum transparency by installing sheer glass walls that rise to the roof. Very large spans are achieved by the use of slender bowstring trusses, held in position by equally slender branching arms. The architects favour islands of check-in counters on the axis of the entrance doors, creating the shortest walking distances from the drop-off area to the departure concourse.

The design and layout, like many recent projects by Aéroports de Paris, place emphasis on the presence of nature amidst the huge expanses of tarmac inevitable at any large airport. Pools and gardens are incorporated in the plans.

In Phase 1 the building extends over two floors, with a central block 402 metres long and 128 metres wide, linked with glazed gangways to a 1,370-metre-long boarding gallery or pier, which is 37 metres wide along its entire length. This will be a spectacular, open space, its cavernous dimensions emphasised by the outward sloping walls.

Road access is provided, in the usual way, on two levels, for departures and arrivals, with 130,000 square metres of parking in the central area, serving over three thousand cars and thirty buses. In Phase 1, provision is made for twenty-eight aircraft to park (international and domestic). Departure halls will have eighty international baggage check-in counters and over a hundred domestic ones.

Estimated construction costs, at 1996 prices, are $317 million for the airport buildings, $25 million for the parking area, and $7.5 million for the viaduct. Passenger statistics are staggering. Phase 1 is designed to handle 20 million passengers, that figure increasing to 70 million with the final phase. Peak international passenger capacity will be 2,800 travellers per hour and 4,300 domestic ones. Completion of the first phase is scheduled for 1999.

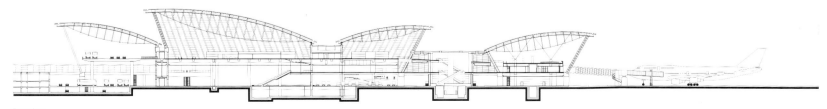

Section

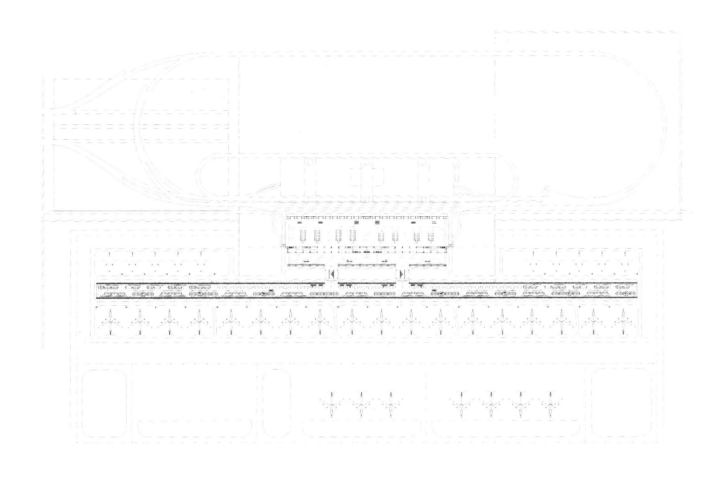

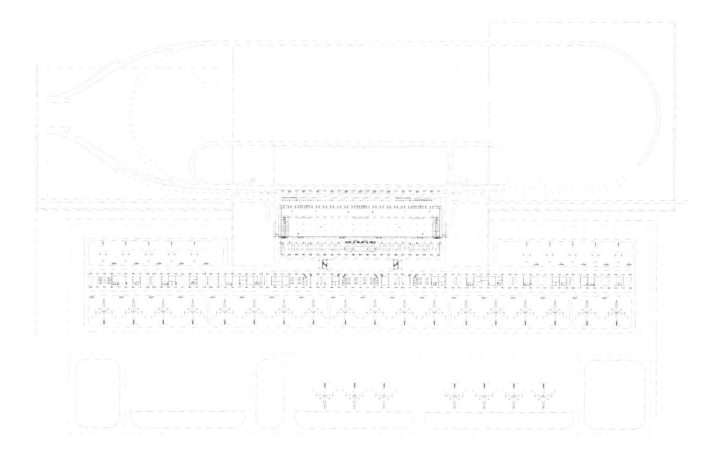

OPPOSITE: Artist's renderings of interior; FROM ABOVE: Upper level plan (departures); ground level plan (arrivals)

Section

North elevation

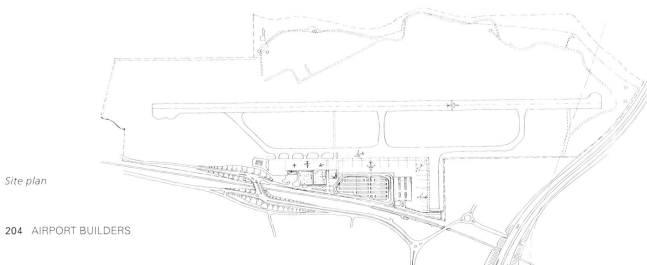

Site plan

SOUTHAMPTON AIRPORT
United Kingdom

The construction cost of this elegant small terminal is held to be, at £6.5 million (£750 per square metre) half that of any previous passenger terminal erected by the British Airports Authority. The graceful appearance of the structure is achieved through its swooping silhouette and sleek, aluminium cladding.

The initial concept came from the engineer, Tony Hunt, who worked on the Channel Tunnel terminal at Waterloo:

> The basic idea is just a cheap and cheerful steel frame. To create the curving roofs we merely suggested taking steel beams and bending them.

Michael Manser, a former president of RIBA, comments:

> It's basically a Dutch barn, with a lean-to on either side: the swept-up roofs are created by bending standard steel beams.

The airport is compact, with departures and arrivals at ground level. There are no airbridges; passengers walk out to the aircraft which stand nearby on the apron. The generous roof overhangs provide some shelter from the rain and by guiding the rainwater through the dip in the roof, the need for gutters is eliminated. Provocatively, the swooping steel beams over the wings stop 5 metres short of the central barn. The load is transferred to thin steel tubes, increasing the sense of daylight flooding in from above.

The lean-to sheds house the check-in and concessions (car rental, shop, bank, cafe and bar) on one side, and the departure lounge, duty free shop and arrivals hall on the other side.

Eastleigh Airport, as it was first known (from the adjacent railway junction), was acquired by Southampton Corporation in 1932 and sold in 1960 to Nat Somers, an entrepreneur with aviation and property interests. At this time it was a grass field. Somers constructed the single 1,720-metre runway. In 1989 the airport was bought by a consortium headed by Peter de Savary, but when this went into receivership in 1990, the airport was sold to the British Airports Authority.

The previous terminal at Southampton, a former Spitfire works, was much prized by regular passengers for its convenience, easy check-in, short walking distances, plentiful car parking nearby and railway station little more than 50 metres from the door. These features have been repeated in the new terminal, a model of stress-free travel, with glass curtain-walls on all sides providing passengers with a reassuring view of the aircraft they are waiting to catch.

Crinkly tin shed it may be, but the finishes are powder-coated, corrugated steel-sheet cladding and grey terrazzo floors, creating a stylish silver and grey livery.

A neat feature of the new terminal is the public observation gallery at its centre. This looks out over the apron and also down into the ticket hall and the lounge at the departure gates, allowing families or friends not only to watch a plane take off but to wave a final goodbye or maintain eye contact, even after passengers have been through security. Special glass virtually eliminates aircraft noise within the terminal.

According to the managing director of the airport, the total cost of £23 million included the renewal of everything except the runway. There are new service buildings, a fire station, two hangars, cargo halls, a control tower as well as extensive landscaping and parking for 1,650 cars.

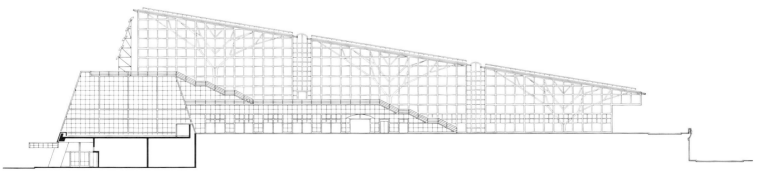

Section

VON GERKAN • MARG & PARTNER

STUTTGART AIRPORT, NEW TERMINAL

Germany

Stuttgart's new terminal, conceived in 1980, is very much a forerunner of the 1990s trend in airport design. In form, it is one of an emerging number of 'supersheds', with a giant roof covering a huge volume of internal space.

Monumental in scale and treatment, it nonetheless has an impressive simplicity of layout. The approach roads and drop-off points are integrated into the building – not simply roads and flyovers set in front of it. The arrival area, as is now the norm, is at ground level, allowing passengers to gather outside and wait, shielded from the elements, for a pick-up vehicle. The upper road, serving the departure hall, is effectively on a terrace over the portico below.

The main roof rises from the roadside towards the apron and the runways: a symbolic suggestion of flight according to the architects. Glass curtain-walls on all sides fill the departures hall with light.

The roof of the 82.8 by 93.6 metre hall is held aloft on a series of twelve steel trees, akin to those at Stansted Airport. Here, the trees spring from a single solid trunk – albeit one composed of four tubes – branching first into clusters of three and then four. The impression is of the spreading form of a great oak, though the straight branches are rather closer in appearance to the more humble cow parsley plant.

The architects' original idea was that the roof should be formed of two layers of glass. These would trap the warmth of the sunlight, which would then be fed through into the hall or transformed into usable energy. As executed, the roof is mainly solid rather than transparent, with long bands of roof lights set between each row of trees. The concourse is best seen at night when the abundance of internal light emphasises the building's loftiness and openness. Moreover, the slenderness of the roof slab is all the more evident.

A wealth of features avoids visual monotony with uplighters in the trees and strong panels of downlighters in the roof which create a warm overall glow.

Inside, passengers ascend to the departure level shops and cafes by way of escalators. The whole idea of a building formed of open terraces linked by symmetrical stairs echoes the ancient Temple of Palestrina which fascinated such architects as Palladio during the Renaissance. Many variations of this form have been made over the centuries, notably a structure not much loved by architects: the monument to Victor Emmanuel in Rome. It is intriguing that one of the most successful (but probably unconscious) modern variants should be in an airport.

The upper level opens out on to a roof terrace which is used to display a series of historic aircraft. Below, the restaurants have a grandstand view of the apron and runway, allowing passengers with time on their hands to eat in comfort and see their inbound aircraft land and arrive at the gate. Part of the appeal of the departure hall is that there is glass on all four sides. Careful inspection reveals the cleaning gantries placed discreetly both inside and out. The architects also extend the indoor terraces along the side walls, providing potential areas for waiting passengers to have some space and peace away from others if they wish, in which to read, doze, make a mobile telephone call, or allow children to play. Unfortunately seats are not provided and so the areas are little used at present.

Stuttgart is exceptional in providing a very large roof terrace overlooking the runways. Von Gerkan takes pleasure in setting the terrace on a massive three-storey podium with an outward sloping face, akin to the 'battered' or buttressed lower wall of a medieval palace or castle.

Elevation

The airbridges are a spectacular feature. They span an apron road the width of a motorway and, in response to this length (which is greater even than at von Gerkan's Hamburg terminal), they are gently arched and stiffened by diagonal braces.

As at Hamburg, von Gerkan opens up the ground level arrivals hall into the departure hall with axially placed escalators and stairs. The strong directional sense is continued by escalators descending on axis to the S-Bahn below, linking the airport with the city centre. The sense of openness is increased by allowing the trees to 'grow' through open balconies which let light penetrate the space below.

Despite the obvious parallels with Stansted Airport, the whole engineering and architectural ethic is very different. Instead of lightness and lean athleticism, there is a delight in mass and visible strength, something much closer in concept and execution to the solidity of nineteenth-century engineering.

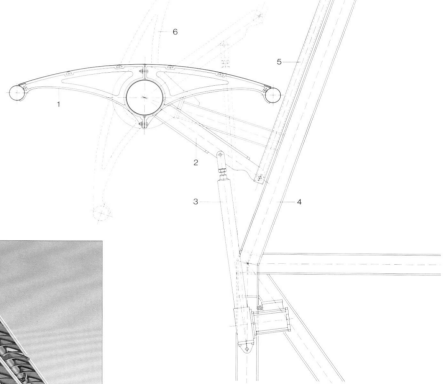

Sunblind components

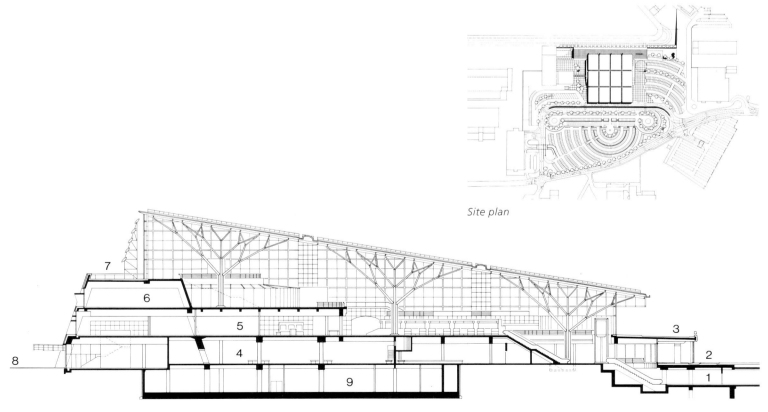

Site plan

Section

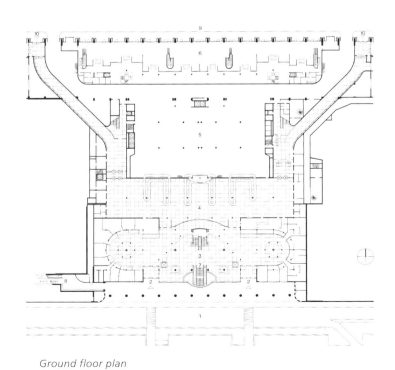

Ground floor plan

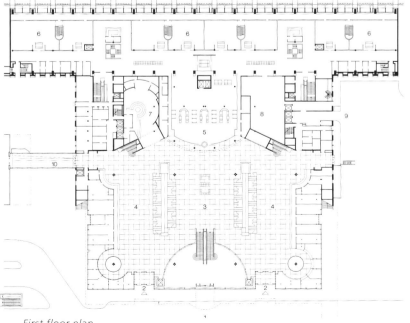

First floor plan

VANCOUVER AIRPORT, NEW TERMINAL
Canada

This airport has a distinctive, colourful personality, intended to provide every passenger with a taste of British Columbian art and culture as well as its awe-inspiring beauty. In 1992, the Vancouver International Airport Authority assumed local control of the airport from Transport Canada. Soon afterwards, an expansion programme was underway, including a new international terminal building, control tower and parallel runway. Construction commenced in May 1994 and was completed in June 1996 at a total cost of $265 million Canadian dollars.

One of the airport authority's stated goals is to minimise costs to airlines. To this end, the new terminal, which opened in 1996, houses Canada's first Common Use Terminal Equipment system (CUTE), allowing airline staff to use any check-in counter on a pay-per-use basis, avoiding check-in counters standing idle for much of the day. Precisely for this reason, the CUTE system reduced the overall building size requirement by thirty per cent, leading to lower costs all round.

The new terminal takes the form of a glass-walled pavilion offering panoramic views of the surrounding sea, mountains and of Vancouver's skyline. Extensive use is made of local stone and wood which are combined with green and blue flooring, providing a much stronger and warmer palette of colours than the normal greys and whites. The steel structure has been designed to allow wide spacing of columns. These mimic trees in a forest, gracefully supporting the roof with branch-like struts.

Designed especially for connecting passengers, the terminal is claimed to be the first of its kind in North America, helping Vancouver compete with other West Coast gateway cities such as Seattle, San Francisco and Los Angeles.

Works by local artists are given pride of place,

notably Bill Reid's massive bronze sculpture, *The Spirit of Haida Gwaii, the Jade Canoe*, on the departures level, and the Musqueam art display, crowned by the world's largest Coast Salish *Spindle Whorl* in the arrivals hall. Inspiration on the retail side came from local attractions such as Whistler resort, Granville Island and Robson Street in Vancouver, and the historic Steveston fishing village in Richmond.

Passenger circulation has presented a particular challenge. By law, international passengers cannot mix with US bound 'transborder' passengers so the terminal is split into two secure sides on the departures level. International passengers check in and depart from gates on the west side while transborder passengers check in and then proceed through US Federal Inspection Services before departing from gates on the east side. This FIS processing, called 'pre-clearance', allows passengers to arrive at any destination in the US without the need for further inspection.

Arriving international and transborder passengers will proceed from their arrival gate via escalators or elevators to a glass-enclosed sky bridge that overlooks departures. Passengers will proceed to the Musqueam Gallery, enjoying views of the sea and mountains before descending two levels by escalator to the Canadian Inspection Services hall and baggage claim area. The reduction of walking distances on arrivals was a prime consideration

There are eight separate baggage systems, including two undertaking automated sorting, mainly due to the range of transfer options, the pre-clearance provisions and the desire to provide a special baggage service direct from the aircraft to cruise ships. Each 'sort system' will laser-read ten-digit bar-coded baggage tags, and automatically route the bags to the appropriate piers for manual loading into carts or containers.

West elevation

East elevation

WASHINGTON NATIONAL AIRPORT, NEW TERMINAL

Washington DC, US

While many of the world's new airports are built on spacious sites, here land is at a premium. This is the ultimate downtown airport, close to the Mall and the great cluster of government buildings. Washington National is a busy airport and its confined site must cater for many passengers who are in a hurry. The airport thrives as a result of its fast connections with the city centre, and has a very large number of domestic flights; international flights, by contrast, arrive at Dulles, some 24 kilometres outside the city.

The new North Terminal is situated between the existing South Terminal of 1941 and the hangars at the north end of the airport. With thirty-five gates, the new facility has a floor area of around 93,000 square metres, including a 488-metre concourse designed to handle sixteen million passengers a year.

The concourse serves three projecting piers – a configuration that allows the maximum number of aircraft to cluster round the terminal. Although symmetrical in layout the piers are uneven in length – the result of the diagonal line of the runway and adjoining taxiways. (Interestingly, the airport has the pattern of three intersecting runways common on wartime aerodromes, rather than adopting the more modern system of parallel runways.)

There are three levels in the new terminal. Ticket counters and departures are at the upper level, the main concourse is in the middle, and the level below contains the baggage claim areas and the 'arrival curb'. From the concourse, the passenger can leave the terminal through an enclosed bridge connecting to the Washington metro and to two newly constructed parking garages, or to the South Terminal.

The design is intended to allow passengers to move in and out of the building without the need for escalators or stairs. The concourse serves as the main 'street' of the building – airy, light and memorable. It is based on the repetition of a 14 by 14 metres, structural steel bay that creates vistas and perspectives akin to those along the aisles and naves of Gothic cathedrals. Each bay is essentially a cross vault supported on four lofty,

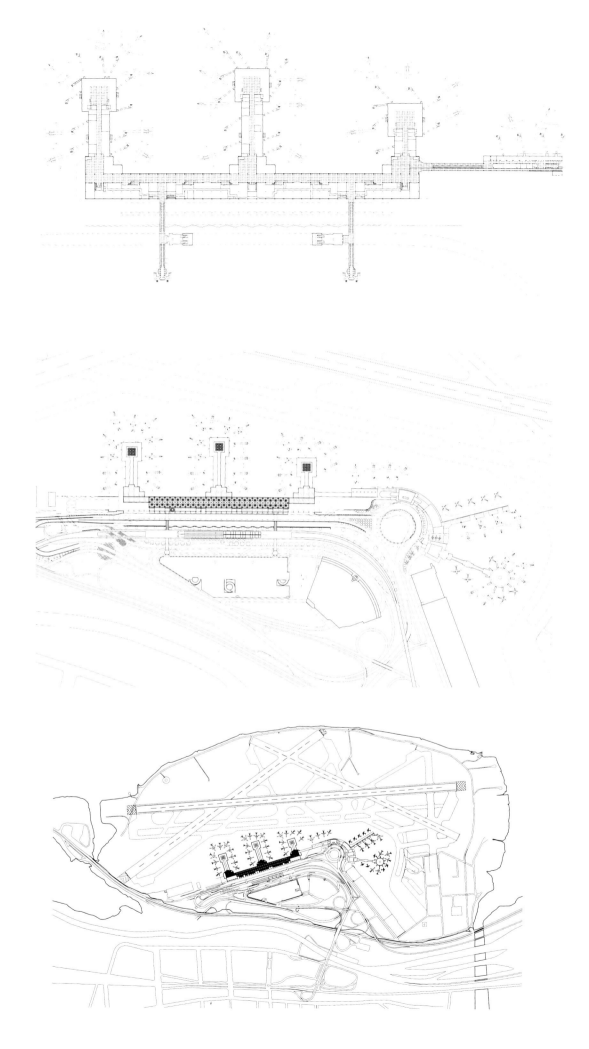

steel pillars inset with an oculus to admit light from above. Just as those cathedral designers strove for increased transparency, so Pelli creates an entire wall of glass in the outside flank.

The Architecture Enhancement Programme (AEP) integrates thirty specially commissioned works of art. These are executed in a wide range of materials – glass, marble, mosaics, terrazzo, cast bronze, copper, hammered aluminium, painted steel, porcelain and paint. Pelli explains:

> We studied many recent and historic alliances of painters, sculptors, architects and artisans. Programmes like the Rockefeller Center in New York City, which has been the benchmark of quality in architectural ornament for decades, and the St Louis train station with its excellent reliefs and bronze fittings were important.

The artworks include ten floor medallions on the main concourse, eleven balustrades overlooking the concourse, five murals, a bridge sculpture, a sunscreen panel on the south wall of the ticket lobby and two glass friezes on the airside of the concourse. The architects worked closely with each of the artists and artisans through both design and fabrication, using both models and drawings.

Pelli's intention is that through the artwork, natural light, comfortable walking distances and uninterrupted views of the airfield, the traveller's experience should be transformed from something tedious into something comfortable and visually stimulating.

OPPOSITE, FROM ABOVE: Roof plan; concourse level plan; site plan; FROM ABOVE: Artist's renderings of interior and exterior

FROM ABOVE: Computer-generated aerial view; roof geometry; elevation of airside centre

ZURICH AIRPORT, AIRSIDE AND LANDSIDE CENTRES

Switzerland

Nicholas Grimshaw & Partners won the competition to design the expansion to Zurich Airport in 1996. The airport already has two terminals and a third remote terminal is currently under construction (won in a separate competition by a Swiss architectural practice).

Grimshaw's project has three major components – landside, airside and parking. The main element, the new Airside Centre, will operate as the node for all three terminals and is intended to serve a growing number of transfer passengers which Zurich is hoping to attract away from London Heathrow and Frankfurt. Chistopher Nash, the project architect, explains:

> Zurich does not have a single internationally known landmark like the Eiffel Tower. Our hope is that the new building which is spectacular in size will become both the gateway and the symbol of the city.

The aim is to create a genuinely grand space. As the sections illustrate, this building will be as tall as the tails of the jumbos on the tarmac outside, its wave roof varying in height from 12 to 18 metres.

The new hall will be at first-floor level: the level of the airbridges. Below is an area in active use by airport vehicles and baggage handling. Construction constraints are enormous and the steel roof structure will be largely prefabricated in order to save time on site.

The new Landside Centre (situated above the mainline train station) and the new Parkhaus C are designed to improve the airport's check-in facilities with an extra sixty desks allocated. Retail facilities here will be doubled.

The Airside Centre will be linked to the new Midfield satellite by a high-speed shuttle train running beneath the taxiways.

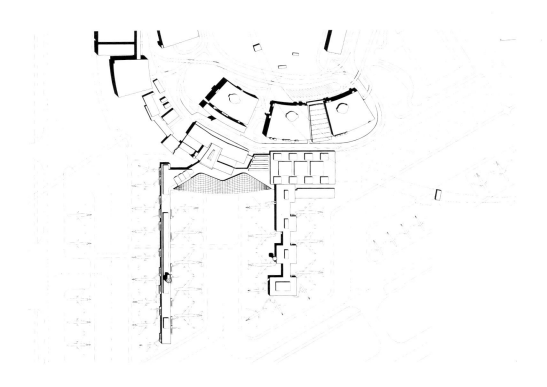

Masterplan

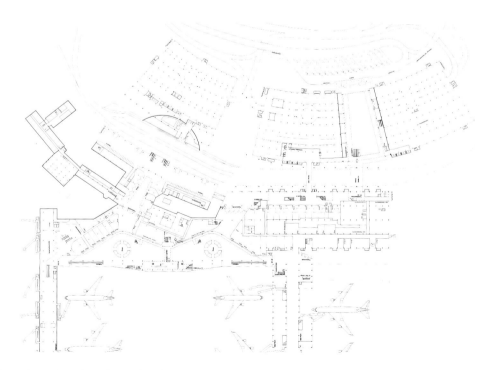

FROM ABOVE: Computer-generated view of interior; plan of main level, airside centre

At present, Zurich Airport is smart but just a little dull. Nash comments:

> The attraction of working at Zurich is that the Swiss have very high standards of finish and construction, compared, say, to Heathrow. But there's also a very strict adherence to rules and regulations. We bring freedom and lateral thinking. Switzerland is currently in recession, though as an outsider you would not know it, and they're looking to us both for economies and flamboyance.

There are, in fact, few better models for a lively transport hub than the typical large Swiss railway station with its numerous restaurants, cafes, bars and shops. In many Swiss towns the railway station is a major focus of town life – where people go to shop and eat. As architects of the new Channel Tunnel terminal at London's Waterloo and Pier 4A at Heathrow, Grimshaw & Partners are in a strong position to understand how to marry the best of the two modes of transport. Nash explains, 'It will have the scale and openness of Stansted but will be more lively as there will be more people.'

Not only will planes taxi past in full view but the light railway will glide past at upper mezzanine level. Often the barrier between airside and landside is complete but here the landside facilities will look into the new airside concourse.

Zurich Airport already boasts a restaurant where, in Nash's words, 'the Swiss take people they want to impress', and the aim is that the new Airside Centre will offer top quality in every price range.

The new 220-metre-long concourse has a wave roof and the intention is that it will be ablaze with light at night, as well as commanding a grandstand view over the aprons by day. The sheer glass walls will be attached to the structure holding up the roof, as in other Grimshaw buildings such as the British Pavilion at the Seville Expo and the Financial Times.

> The difference is that the environment at a major airport is much harsher in terms of both noise and pollution. We're using triple glazing, and as it faces west a system of louvres, probably glass, to prevent dazzle in the evening. The louvres will move with the sun, diminishing but not cutting out the view.

Switzerland is prone to heavy rains, and to prevent flash flooding, a law requires large new buildings to retain rainwater that falls on the roof, rather than discharge it directly into drains, releasing it over a period of time.

Building was scheduled to start in 1998, with construction of the new Airside Centre due for completion in 2001 and of the Landside Centre in 2003.

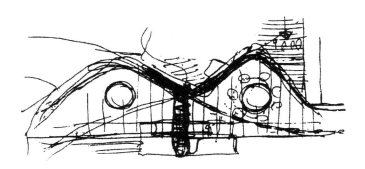

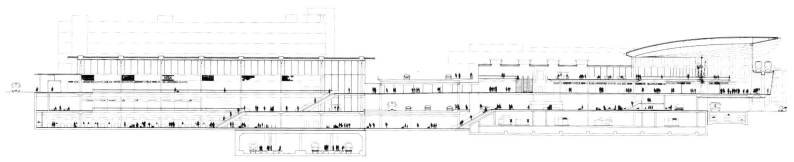

RIGHT AND BELOW: Sketch by Grimshaw; section through landside and airside centres

INDEX